THE STOCKTON LECTURES

FOUNDED IN MEMORY OF ISSACHAR J. GOLDSTON
Born Stockton-on-Tees, England, 1884
Died Warren, Ohio, U.S.A., 1961

PRODUCTIVITY

AND AMENITY

THE STOCKTON LECTURES, 1973

PRODUCTIVITY AND AMENITY

Achieving a Social Balance

EDITED BY
MICHAEL BEESLEY

CROOM HELM LONDON

CRANE, RUSSAK NEW YORK

Published in Great Britain 1974

© 1974 by Michael Beesley

Croom Helm Ltd
2–10 St. Johns Road, London SW 11

ISBN 0–85664–145–6

Published in the United States by
Crane, Russak & Company Inc.
52 Vanderbilt Avenue
New York, N.Y. 10017

ISBN 0–8448–0269–7

Library of Congress Catalog Card No 73–91528

Printed and bound in Great Britain by
Redwood Burn Ltd.
Trowbridge and Esher.

CONTENTS

Foreword

In 1952 my wife and I came to England for the first time. After the usual tourist visits to Westminister Abbey and The Tower and while carrying the usual tourist outfit of camera and guidebook, we went to King's Cross Station. 'Two tickets to Stockton-on-Tees,' I requested in my Mid-Western American voice. 'You mean two tickets for Stratford-on-Avon,' the clerk replied, 'where Shakespeare was born.' I responded, 'No. Two tickets for Stockton-on-Tees where my father was born.' That incident suggests the origin of these lectures – a son's interest in his father's birthplace and an American's readiness to educate the British.

Twenty years later I returned to England for a six month sabbatical from my job as a professional corporate manager – and noted that Stockton-on-Tees had greatly declined in amenity not only from my father's descriptions of its pastoral quality in his youth but even from my own first visit. (Indeed, Stratford-on-Avon had also declined in amenity.)

At The London Graduate School of Business Studies, I explored how differently the Americans and the British have tried to reconcile the quantity and quality of our lives. Although corporate social responsibility has been more widely expected in the United States than in Britain, government planning and responsibility are less expected in the United States.

My father, an architect converted into a retailer by the

Great Depression, managed to generate not only profit but social benefit and fun after he 'entered trade'. Thwarted from designing beautiful structures, he instead built a business that was regarded with respect and fondness by his employees, neighbours, suppliers, and customers. Thus, these lectures are named after his birthplace in memory of an Englishman who, by doing well while doing good in a small Ohio town, demonstrated to his community that there can be a social as well as an economic rationale for business activity — that a man can live greatly in business as well as in a profession or in government service.

ELI GOLDSTON

Preface

This volume contains the Stockton Lectures on 'Productivity and Amenity: Achieving a Social Balance', delivered at the London Business School before an invited audience from industry, government and the academic world between January and April 1973.

These lectures were generously sponsored by Eli Goldston, President of Eastern Gas and Fuel Associates in Boston, after spending a sabbatical year at the School. The lectures are named after his father's birth-place at Stockton-on-Tees, and the subject chosen for the series is one in which Mr. Goldston himself has always had a deep personal interest. We are very much in his debt.

We are grateful for the contributions of the distinguished contributors, Peter Walker, the Secretary of State for Trade and Industry (Chapters 2 and 6), Lord Zuckerman (Chapter 4) and Philip Nind (Chapter 5) and our colleague Michael Beesley who not only contributed to the lecture series (Chapter 3) but also added an introductory essay (Chapter 1) and saw the volume through the press.

We are, in addition, grateful to all those who saw through the arrangements for the pleasant evenings enjoyed by the speakers and their audience after the lectures.

R. J. BALL
Principal

ONE

The Context of Social Responsibility in Business

M.E. BEESLEY

The theme of the lectures, of achieving a balance between the social requirements for enhancing both productivity and amenity, was born of the coincidence of Eli Goldston's own concern and work in this area in the USA and the upsurge of interest in corporate responsibility on this side of the Atlantic, itself manifest in the London Business School's teaching and research. Since the lectures were delivered, public debate has been stimulated by the UK Government's White Paper on company law reform[1] which, alongside specific proposals for increasing information about company transactions, and banning insider trading, raised the broader question of the social responsbility of companies. Specific proposals have yet to be devised. These lectures are thus, one hopes, a contribution to the difficult task of coaxing viable, practical measures of reform from a wide ranging debate.

The issues of social responsibility for companies are remarkably difficult to sort out in a way helpful to action. The White Paper indicates this clearly, while certainly raising many relevant issues. In writing of the 'public responsibility of the company', the Government, like most commentators, by implication finds it much easier to state what it does not involve than what it does.

11

It argues that directors must do their best for shareholders, but that nowadays the aim cannot only be 'the
simple one of immediate profitability'. However, few
have supposed that even the most dedicated profit-
seekers ever suffered from this degree of myopia. So
will *enlightened* self-interest (profit-seeking) suffice?
Apparently not, because while it is true that 'boards of
directors can and do have regard to such matters as the
interests of customers, of employees and of the general
public, since these matters bear on the reputation and
well-being of the company as well as upon short-term
profit', it is important to 'set criteria for judging whether
in any particular case they have done so to an acceptable
degree'. The Paper discusses the possibility of a Code of
Conduct, but, apart from being in doubt about its
positive content, points out that to be effective, it must
from a company's viewpoint be binding on its competitors also and, thus, be capable of enforcement. An
analogy might seem to be the City Take-over Code and
Panel, but 'the Panel has of course the sanctions of the
Stock Exchange behind it, and it is not at present easy to
see what counterpart might exist in relation to the
general run of industrial decisions.' Thus, apart from
legislating for specific abuses by companies or executives,
the most concrete steps seem to the Government to be to
increase the requirements of a company to report its
actions, for example the company's performance on the
health and safety of its employees, or consumer com-
plaints, and in conducting industrial relations. The White
Paper at the same time sees needs to strengthen the
position of particular interest groups in the company,
namely the employees, to involve them more closely in
company affairs, and the shareholders, by encouraging

the trend towards appointing non-executive directors to 'discharge the stewardship function' and by harnessing the influence of the large institutional shareholders to this end. Thus the choice of *means* to effect a shift of concern by boards is left a very open question. Rather paradoxically, the strengthening of specific interests' ability to influence decisions would of course make more difficult the job of the board at large in holding a 'just' balance in the public interest.

We may therefore discern problems of *identifying* the items which should go into the looked for social balance, which involves identifying also the interested parties who will benefit or lose; *evaluating* these items so that the claims of the parties can be reconciled or if necessary offset one against the other in response to agreed principles; of *choosing means* of implementing social aims; and of *monitoring and enforcing* decisions. Clearly also there is a considerable technical problem in relating cause and effect and predicting the outcome of actions. It turns out, then, that the issues are capable of being classified in ways similar to that used for most decision-making processes. This may be a useful way for the reader to organise his thoughts. The lectures were not, however, intended to follow such a theme; they were instead meant to explore in as free-ranging a manner as possible the underlying considerations in formulating policies.

The debate, moreover, has a much more general significance even than that of choosing wise policies to reconcile productivity and amenity given, broadly, the present structure of industrial society. In the surge of debate about social purposes of industry, it may be argued, it is Western-style modern capitalism which is in

process of being judged. Can it be reconciled with, or
adapted to, new social demands for improving the quality
of life? Capitalism, necessarily changing in character, has
indeed essentially survived the stresses of mass unemployment and the growth of economic nationalism and
increasing State involvement in directing economies. But
current doubts concern the preservation of non-economic
values, and, as Peter Walker implies, apologists for
modern capitalism seem to have had little success in
preventing the growth of scepticism about its likely
performance here. Thus a restatement of the functions
of, and justification for, modern capitalism seems timely.
This Peter Walker does in his contributions in Chapters 2
and 6. This is a question of alternative means of
economic organisation also: if not modern capitalism,
what else?

Economic growth may be antipathetic to amenity, but
it also provides the means to improve it. Peter Walker
draws a comparison between modern capitalism and
communism highly favourable to the former. Economic
systems are to be judged by their results in terms of
producing wealth, yielding a desirable quality of life and
in securing widespread assent and participation. Because
of its emphasis on innovation, reconciliation of scale with
flexibility, and its pragmatic attitudes, capitalism is a
superior producer of wealth. All modern technology
underlying economic systems produces problems of
amenity (a theme also stressed by Lord Zuckerman), and
capitalism now has specific deficiencies which can and
should be remedied. This, he argues, may call for a new
kind of partnership between government, banking, and
the two sides of industry. There is certainly, however, a
need more clearly to define government's role and

perhaps to codify company responsibilities with respect
to social obligations. This is an idea mooted again in the
White Paper: and the nature, content, and possible
working of a social audit for a company such as might
accompany a code is the subject of the last section of my
own paper (Chapter 3). All lectures are indeed concerned
with defining the government's role, and I consider the
place and prospect of quantifying social concern in it,
which draws comment from Lord Zuckerman. Modern
business, it is generally agreed, has also a positive social
role, as for example in providing for job enlargement, as
Peter Walker stresses, or in inventing new social responses
to needs, and proving a resource for providing the
management skills necessary to translate social aims into
effective action. Even if modern capitalism can succeed,
with enlightened government, in responding to social
needs in the technical and economic sense – and the
lectures are, on the whole, optimistic here – it still
requires a clearer moral basis, Peter Walker argues, to
retain assent. He sees the need for more explicit support
in industrial action for values such as individual opportunity, self-development and security.

That the productivity versus amenity debate is placed
in the context of the merits of rival economic systems
will seem to some readers an interesting revival of
arguments of the fifties and sixties. Then, it will be
recalled, there was far less consensus about a company's
general obligations beyond profit-making. Nearly all
recent discussions of social responsibility seem obliged to
refer to Professor Milton Friedman's famous defence of
the notion that social responsibility of business is to seek
profits and not to seek to serve other social ends except
as decreed by government in democratically-arrived-at

decisions. Most commentators now dismiss the notion
summarily; and the reader will note a reflection of this in
some following chapters, although there is, as seen
already, considerable stress on the government's role as
definer of social aims. But it is important to remember
that the notion was, and is still, part of a very serious
argument holding that property rights, as for instance
manifest in company shareholding, and, more fundamentally, the right to engage freely in economic activity are
necessary (admittedly not sufficient) conditions for the
maintenance of Western-style political freedom. The
debate is, therefore, not simply a matter of the competitive merits of economic systems, their manner of
coping with technological advance, or their relative
responsiveness to changing ideas about amenity, but of
sustaining a uniquely favourable framework for individual
expression. Capitalism's better economic performance,
while marked, is a secondary matter, important because it
serves political freedom. This view admits the imperfec-
tions of markets and — contrary to widespread ideas
about it — the need for State intervention to correct
social disbenefits not reflected in them. But it is
profoundly suspicious of centralised government, and
therefore hostile to its growth, seeing this as indirectly
sapping the essential economic freedoms. This is not the
place fully to enter this debate, but I must admit myself
to having sufficient respect for it to classify my own
position (I cannot of course speak for the other lecturers)
as perhaps 'neo-Friedmanite'. Thus I argue for a clear
governmental responsibility in declaring social aims;
careful scrutiny by governments of the basis for intervention to secure them; development of cost-benefit analysis,
which is one form of check for the propriety of

government actions; and preparedness by the government to be critical of the means of intervention at its disposal — with a decided preference for those allowing more private adaptive actions. Some of this, at least, the reader will see, chimes in with Lord Zuckerman's points about the role of technologists in social choice and about the analysis of social actions. Partly also because I have a suspicion of the managerial efficiency of very large-scale organisations, I would further argue that the government, in responding actively to new social purposes, as it certainly must do, should also be aware of the need to review its existing scope; it should consciously aim to substitute the more effective intervention for the less. This, in turn, requires a willingness to relinquish powers, a challenging aim for all governments.

But how do, or should, social purposes such as the desire to protect the environment in certain ways get recognised and become candidates for social action? This, Lord Zuckerman implies, is the more important precisely because developing technology has been so powerful, throughout the world, in shaping desires for economic growth and providing the potential means for safeguarding amenity. Threats to the environment are often easily perceived in principle, but their significance is much less easily grasped and appreciated; some threats are very remote, and some developments may be deeply ambiguous for human welfare. None of the lectures produces an answer, and this is perhaps the most interesting and, probably, important issue to be addressed in future debate. How can we improve the processes of recognition and definition of, for example, potential environmental damage or, indeed, improvement? This is an essential prerequisite of planning effectively, whether at government or company level. Most debate has taken place on the improvement of evaluating actions – for example, how to increase public participation directly or indirectly – rather than on the generation of potential action. A proper examination of this question will have to consider the roles of the press, political organisations and voluntary movements as well as those, such as scientists, to which the lectures give some attention. The lectures do however show a considerable confidence in the democratic processes to throw up relevant aims, while seeing a need to increase channels of communication, and to stimulate the expression of scientific and professional opinion. Business itself is also an important source of potential and social reform.

In the choice of action, Lord Zuckerman argues, social priorities cannot be left to scientific (or by extension, indeed, any expert) opinion, but are the proper concern of political processes, a view to which all the lectures explicitly or implicitly assent. But there is much scope for further analysis of alternatives too, even though the ground here has been better tilled. There are many ways of legitimising choice of action for governments – from referenda to the extreme of calling a general election; or, in on-going government, from ad hoc enquiry to fully qualified social cost-benefit analysis. Their relative merits and fit to circumstances constitute a useful field for further enquiry. Socially oriented companies have also a range of possible techniques for legitimising action, some of which are taken up in my lecture.

Fundamental to all progress in identifying and acting upon the problems thrown up by reconciling production with amenity is education. Mr. Nind, in Chapter 5, argues the need for improved educational provision both for the perception and resolution of problems of social responsibility. The quality of leadership is crucial, in his view, and this in turn requires educational processes which will produce a larger number of talented and appropriately educated people. He explores the tensions between this desideratum and the prevailing egalitarian trend in education, and he argues the changes needed to produce 'more and better' educated people, in which modular forms of instruction, flexibility in the timing of educational effort and, above all, continuing educational experience are important. Corporate education is but part of this process, but the principal business educational institutions, Mr. Nind argues, will not only have great influence in shaping attitudes to social responsibility in board rooms, but should also be a process for the reconciliation of conflicts arising from economic progress. In the wider educational processes, he argues the case for integrating the environmental perspective into the education of students at all levels.

From this review of the contents of the lectures, necessarily somewhat selective and condensed, it will be seen that their ambition is to raise, and in part to clarify, issues, rather than settle them. They do not pretend to be comprehensive, and there are conspicuous gaps. Perhaps the most obvious is analysis of the implications of the discussions for practical company management. Suppose, for example, a company proposes to follow policies which protect amenity but which cannot be wholly rationalised in terms of company self-interest, however imaginatively conceived. (Much can be done by companies to serve both their own and externally oriented purposes simultaneously and it may be that in the intensified search for these opportunities lies a major way to progress, but this is unlikely to be adequate in social terms.) What will be the implications for management processes? The company has at least two sets of problems here – the satisfaction of the interest groups – for example, shareholders, management itself, employees, retired employees, customers who may have legitimate claims for attention in policy changes; and the quality of decision-making in the company. The first is a familiar problem even with financial decisions, and social concern adds a new dimension that raises again the question of to whom and in what form is top management responsible. The second is perhaps less familiar but none the less important for the large firm. Adding concerns for amenity preservation to normal commercial motivation complicates, perhaps severely, the making of decisions and, more important, the problems of delegation of authority, holding subordinates to account, and deciding on relative personal achievement. A management consensus might be easier to define and act upon were management professionalised to a much larger degree than it is now, for professions indeed incorporate standards and ethics expressly to modify and define the limits of commercial activity. But the prospect for organised professionalism in management in that sense is remote, and many would say (Friedman among them) inimical to enterprise and therefore to deeper freedoms. At best, cautious experiment seems to be called for.

In the practice of reconciling productivity and amenity at company level, the UK has much to learn from the US in particular. Prominent among the practitioners has been Eli Goldston himself, whose experience at Eastern Gas & Fuel Associates is in part at least a matter of record[2] and is referred to later. He has conveyed in the foreword something of his optimism for the outlook for the socially responsible company, and we were fortunate indeed that one social innovation – the sabbatical for presidents between contracts – brought him to the London Business School at just the right time. We at the School are greatly in his debt, not only for suggesting and supporting the Stockton Lectures, but also for focusing an important sphere of interaction between the School and business.

He also brought to the School a specific notion about measuring society's welfare to which I refer in my lecture, and about which a word of explanation is appropriate here. The nation-wide performance of an economy is usually measured by national accounting techniques which sum up all that is produced *and* is the subject of market transactions in the economy. If, and only if, an output is priced – either directly by the market or by resources which are themselves priced (by wage payments for example) does it rank for inclusion. [There are of course many adjustments for external trade, capital consumption etc. which need not concern us here.] From the point of view of judging whether a nation is *really* getting better off or not, these measures, useful as they are, have two glaring deficiencies. First, important outputs which people certainly value are not the subject of market transactions and thus are 'wrongly' omitted. Housewives' services are a classic example; and so is leisure (if it increases, other things being equal, measured 'national income' will fall). Second, some things are produced which people would on the whole, prefer to be without, like pollution or armaments or blight. These can hardly be called beneficial; nevertheless they may, directly or indirectly, be counted into output.

The 'Measurement of Economic Welfare' to which I refer is an attempt to correct some of the more notable of these errors of omission and commission, like social cost-benefit analysis, it should be judged not solely upon its technical content but rather upon its merits as an aid to decision making and in particular to guiding governmental action, and it is in this way that I present it in my lecture.

NOTES

1 Department of Trade & Industry, Company Law Reform, CMNd. 5391 HMSO, London, July 1973.
2 For example: Eli Goldston, 'Corporate Social Responsibility and Management Behavior', *Journal of Contemporary Business*, Winter 1973.
   This article is based on Mr. Goldston's three Benjamin F. Fairless Memorial Lectures presented at the Graduate School of Industrial Administration at Carnegie-Mellon University.

TWO

The Changing Roles of Government and Business

P. WALKER

For most of this century the world has been dominated by the ideological struggle between capitalism and communism. I believe we are now entering a phase in world history when Adam Smith's concept of capitalism and Karl Marx's concept of communism will become matters of historical interest. We are well aware in a democratic society such as our own, that those who advocate the advantages of a free enterprise system have as part of their aspirations a range of social objectives shared by many of the more enlightened people in communist countries. The goals are similar. Disagreement is now primarily about the means. Capitalism and communism today are becoming less conflicting ideologies and, more, *alternative mechanisms*.

The purist arguments for capitalism no longer apply. Capitalism has a contribution to make, but in a changed form. Those of us who seek for our society advantages of a free enterprise system must examine objectively a number of major spheres and eradicate the disadvantages. We must realise, in our provision of incentives, in our organisation of the taxation system and in our examination of industrial relations, that capitalism of the latter part of the twentieth century is a system in which

23

the proprietor and the manager are no longer synony-
mous as they were in the nineteenth century. We must
realise that, with a younger generation better educated
than any generation in the history of mankind, there is a
need to develop rapidly a rational solution to the
employer/employee partnership and recognise that the
trends are towards partnership rather than enlightened, or
in some cases unenlightened, paternalism. Modern capitalism has an increasing need both in Government and
industry to see that the results of its productivity are
directed to eliminating poverty, whereas historical nineteenth century capitalism was able to a substantial degree
to ignore it. Capitalism must use technology in such a
way that future generations are not obliged to spend the
greater part of their waking hours within factory walls
doing work of little mental or spiritual satisfaction.
Likewise throughout the communist world the weak-
nesses of that system are becoming more and more
recognised: the failure to provide that wider diversity of
choice which is so essential to the quality of life, the
failure to encourage individual enterprise which the
human race naturally demands and responds to. Its
immense spiritual weakness is reflected best in its
inflexibility and its demands for the elimination of basic
human rights, and the failure of a system stated to be a
system of public ownership to provide the public with
any real sense of participation. The two major economic
systems of the twentieth century are therefore in the
process of changing and the citizens of both have good
cause to welcome that change.

    We have reached a position, both in the United States
and Britain, where there is a multitude of young people
who look upon commerce and trade with a hostility

almost identical to that of the landed aristrocrats in the nineteenth century. They are wrong. There is no doubt in my mind that a man of goodwill, conscious of his responsibilities, who devotes a great part of his life to providing leadership in running companies can and does contribute as much to the wellbeing of his fellow men as any social worker. For it is such men that provide the means of eliminating poverty. It is such men who provide the range of goods and services that makes life itself more interesting, full and fascinating. It is such men who in the past have made possible improvements in the standards of living and housing of a large majority in the developed countries of the world. And it is such men who are going to provide the means of removing poverty and mal-nutrition in the developing countries. In the decades that lie ahead, to opt out of applying one's skills to the organisation of production and the provision of services could well be to opt out of providing a much fuller and richer life for the majority of mankind.

The worst side of capitalism has been the sight of the capitalist exploiting selfishly the means of production regardless of other considerations. It is the task of Government to see that the impetus of capitalism is harnessed to the interests of all the people. Capitalism should not be regarded as the means for a few to get rich without regard to the needs and hopes of the majority of people. Management and workers are increasingly de-manding a more balanced share of the rewards of successful enterprise. Management and labour, recognis-ing its power, are demanding greater participation in ownership. It is true that a great part of the population, through the institutions of banks, insurance companies or trade union funds, participate on a massive scale in the ownership of industry. But this is a form of ownership not directly related to their own experience and activities, and therefore a form of ownership less satisfying in the impact it makes on the multitude of individuals concerned.

In the context, therefore, of modern capitalism, I want to discuss some aspects of the role of the state. First, the state is best equipped to assess the national opportunity in the context of the world as a whole. If one judges the relative success in commercial terms of the major industrial nations of the world during the post-war period, it can be argued that the most successful countries are those countries where the state, the banking system and both sides of industry have joined together to agree upon the international opportunities available and to take advantage of them. Perhaps in post-war Britain we should have concentrated more on creating a genuine partnership between Government, banking and both sides of industry with the objective of providing the maximum industrial economic expansion for the nation as a whole.

Secondly the Government must see that commercial activities are fair, open and just. The framework of company law must be correct. Practices which give an unfair advantage to a few to the detriment of the many, such as the practice of insider dealing, must be stopped. If major sections of the economy are to merge or the efficient firm is to take over the inefficient, it should be done on the basis of full information about the likely advantages and disadvantages for the interests directly concerned and the community as a whole. I cannot over-emphasise the importance for the working of capitalism that it should be open, free and based on integrity. If it is not open and free, wrong decisions will be made, but, more important, it will forfeit public confidence. This is why I want to tighten up the laws in a number of spheres of company legislation.*

Thirdly, Government has a responsibility for the quality of life itself. It is absurd to continue a system where an industrialist can create a bad environment for the sake of profit. The costs of removing the scars of pollution must be borne by those who create them. It must be wrong that industry should be free to ignore the desirability of good physical planning and it is the duty of Government and local government to see that the nation, particularly one as densely populated as our own, pursues the most enlightened policies towards its physical environment. It must also be wrong for industry to be allowed to ignore the long-term trends in energy and raw material resources, and it is the duty of Governments to see that the interests of future generations are protected by rational and sensible policies.

A fourth task of Government is to pursue within the boundaries of its country, and thereafter internationally, policies that tackle both regional and international imbalance. It must be right within a nation such as ours, to provide incentives and encouragement to use, where necessary, controls to see that each region of the country benefits from increasing prosperity, and no one region becomes an area of declining standards because of its historic connection with a declining industry.

Fifthly Government has a duty to see, and this duty in combination with private enterprise itself to see, that

*Editor's note: as seen in Chapter 1, the Government's White Paper on Company Law Reform appeared in July 1973.

the economic system encourages the fullest application of the talents and abilities of each individual. One cannot help but be concerned when vast industrial companies develop private bureaucracies which stifle enterprise. Young men get locked into the career structure of huge organisations, their escape blocked by mortgages, pension rights and the need to support the children. Their road to a position where the vigour and enterprise of youth could be used is inevitably a long one, so that by the time they reach such a position the vigour and enterprise have been ironed out of their system and they present to the world the smooth face of the Corporation man. In the past it could have been argued that industry suffered from a drain of the brightest of our people into the public administration of a vast colonial empire. This was at least a drain that made a very considerable contribution to the development of the world as a whole. The equivalent today is that some of the most able and enterprising are attracted to dealing situations and not into industry and management where they are desperately needed. It is in these circumstances that the state has a role to modify the rules of the game so that people of ability have every incentive to apply those talents where they are most needed.

If these are some aspects of the role of the state, what of the role of industry itself? Firstly, it is to be efficient and make a profit for Britain (that is a social responsibility no less than a business one). Secondly, it is not to pollute (you would expect me to put that high on the list having been the first Secretary of State for the Environment in the world). Thirdly, it is to ensure that it looks after and assists its employees: to develop and apply new talents to the full and to provide opportunities for satisfaction at work. Fourthly it is not to cheat or mislead but to give service to consumers large and small and, one may add — when domestic appliances break down — to admit mistakes and rectify them; and it is to support national objectives. I am thinking particularly of the regional balance of employment, of the need to control inflation, of the essential re-training in this age of quickly changing jobs and of the balance of payments.

Society is a series of mutual duties and obligations between individuals. **Social** harmony is achieved and social welfare promoted when the individuals who make up society fully accept these duties and obligations. From the point of view of the capitalist system this means that it must be humane and equitable as well as efficient and dynamic. Managers in business have a basic duty to look after their employees; to provide, as far as they are able, suitable employment; not to waste the talents of any of their employees and particularly not of the bright ones whose talents can help others; indeed, not to waste people. It is absurd that countless thousands can protest at the noise of an aircraft occasionally flying overhead whereas the volume of noise suffered in some of our factories is both continuous and much more damaging. The provision of the best possible environmental conditions in places where many will spend a large proportion of their waking lives must be an essential of a modern capitalist system. We should be concerned to see that every effort is made to create a general sense of community by social, sporting and any other facilities.

Industry consists of people. If people's jobs are dull, tedious and uninteresting, then you cannot expect them to take an interest in their work or the well-being of the firm. If people's work gives them no responsibility then

they will not act responsibly. If they feel that they have
no control or influence over their work situation then
they will, if dissatisfied, try to control it through conflict.
That can help no one. Everybody needs a sense of
satisfaction and of achievement. This will mean that from
now onwards management will have to examine constantly the potential for job enlargement and methods by
which jobs on the dreary assembly line are transformed
into being part of a group endeavour. I sometimes think
that trade union organisers, because of the pressures upon
them, become mesmerised with the question of wages.
The best of them are concerned also with job satisfaction.
They should also be concerned with the prosperity of the
firm as a whole; it is better to work for a prosperous firm
than a declining one. This means they should look out for
opportunities and prod the management if it is missing
those opportunities. All this is very much in the interests
of their members.

We have however, massive and challenging problems,
not only in this country but in the world. We simply
cannot allow our economic growth to flag, with con-
sequent effects on the quality of our lives, while we stand
on ceremony and bow towards nineteenth century views
of the proper division of responsibility between management, labour and Government. We must recognise that
we all as individuals, and as representatives of one or
other group, share goals and interests which are vital to us
all. If we can translate this ideal into dynamic practical
action, we can declare our generation free of dogma and
worthy to succeed.

THREE

The Criteria for Social Perfomance

M.E. BEESLEY

Introduction

As Eli Goldston reminded us in a lecture at the London
Business School last year, it is important to attempt to
quantify social concern because it focuses choice, makes
us think in practical terms, and provides yardsticks for
judging progress – and thus provides stimulus to further
effort. So much of recent discussion of social responsibilities has been unsatisfactory because it has been
vaguely formulated. To put issues in terms of economic
growth versus a good environment, or growth versus
conservation, as is often done, is remarkably unhelpful,
though it provides good sport for academics. For one
thing, in our duopolistic competitive political system no
party will actually propose such a trade-off; too many
hostages are given to growth. For another, such a precise
choice is hardly within the technical competence of
Governments: performance versus promise on growth
have diverged greatly. Most important, however, significant trade-offs in effect have been made: successive
British governments have been revealed to sacrifice
growth to environmental ends. One thinks of the decision
to choose Maplin rather than Cublington as a site for the

31

third London Airport, the whole group of measures to
preserve the amenities of town life like the Clean Air Act
and the subsidy of urban transport through investment
grants; the green belt policies; the commitment to
lessening many of the nuisances caused by traffic; and
extending the principles of compensation for the injuries
effected by public investment. Growth has been revealed
sacrificed to other ends too, of course; *I* would say, to
technological patriotism (Concorde) or, much more
defensibly, by giving regional aid to poor areas in the
country. But one imagines that the disinterested outsider
would say, looking over the last few years that, in the UK
social concern has been shown to be growing.

The issues now seem to me to be more practical: what
areas of concern should be selected for more attention,
how does one choose between them; what instruments of
policy are there; how does one choose between them; and
how does one check on progress and ensure good new
ideas get seriously considered? Those attuned to business
school thinking will immediately recognise here the germ
of a systems approach to social concern. I shall discuss in
particular the place of quantification of social concern,
and the problem of sorting out what should be the roles
of Government, those of business collectively, and what
are those of individual companies. I shall assume that a
reasonable national goal is to apply resources to social
purposes in such a way as either to reduce the resources
sacrificed for given social ends, or to gain greater social
pay-offs for a given sacrfice of resources. This is a useful
approach partly because it makes the trade-offs more
explicit, and therefore more amenable to political and
public control, and partly because it will tend to make
Government more effective in dealings with other

Governments. (I assume here that a government that wishes to give a lead in matters of the international environment is better placed if it is more, rather than less, well organised in the choices it makes at home.)

II The Problems Facing Governments

I start by assuming social purposes are known; so I have initially to dodge the question of what at any given time social concerns should be. It is a fascinating question how particular concerns like pollution, conservation, noise avoidance, job rewards, visual amenity or safety become established as desirable social ends having some call for our attention. But I am most concerned first with the quality of response government and business makes to known social purposes.

Effective action depends on disentangling objectives. Unfortunately a great deal of support for environmental ends is opportunistic. 'Protection of the environment' can be called in to aid any progressive or retrogressive cause; it is a rallying cry, a cover for many strange bedfellows. 'Environment' is a particularly useful term for those wishing to mask real objectives. Since it is defined in O.E.D. as simply 'surroundings', one can see how easily it can mean all things to all men. In approaching the question of 'conservation', for example, it is important rigorously to test the question of how far we need to preserve an industry's capacity, using a test which clearly distinguishes the interests of those in the industry from those of other parties. Such a discussion has been initiated by Derek Ezra's recent article on the prospects of a world energy crisis.[1] One may well wish to argue

about his conclusions; but the approach – of assessing
the case for supporting UK coal production by examining
the need for 'insurance' against world changes in fuel
supply – was surely a correct one. Thus we must define
what it is we are trying to preserve and enhance, predict
the effects of our actions and examine alternative
methods of securing these.

One part of faith in this approach is that a commitment to analyse in turn clarifies objectives. But I must
admit that, in our system, being explicit has its draw-
backs in the sense that organising support for a policy
change can be inhibited by too clear a specification of
objectives and analysis of consequences. The clearer they
are, the more one is likely to encounter organised
opposition, rational or not. Nevertheless this problem can
be tackled too. If governments are to be more explicit in
advancing social ends, they will increasingly have to
provide explicit means to compensate those adversely
affected by change. This is one of the reasons why the
current move to extend compensation in the field of
injurious affection[2] is so welcome, for it widens the
scope for manoeuvre in satisfying social needs.

But in practical terms, analysis of effects of pursuing
social goals, even if the goals are initially quite widely
formulated, may soon indicate that concentration on
specific and relatively few goals is what is required. This
is illustrated by the experience of the Urban Motorways
Committee, of which I was a member. It set off in 1969
to explore the consequences for the urban environment
of road investment. With the help of consultants we were
able to narrow down the wide field of impact to four
significant ones – noise, severance, visual intrusion and
nuisance during construction. Of these the importance of

severance – the disruption to the local community, particularly, had not been fully appreciated before the work began. Recommendation of suitable action was accordingly made more manageable.[3]

Given the social ends to be pursued, and commital to economy in their pursuit, some form of social cost benefit analysis, whether explicit or implicit, becomes inevitable. Unchecked enthusiasm for a pursuit of an end such as, for example, safety in motor cars may be disfunctional. A very interesting demonstration of this has recently emerged from the USA. It will be recalled that there are two phases of legislative reaction to the Nader campaign for safety in cars; the first to 1970 which has already resulted in revised specifications for cars and the second, the projected phase up to 1975, which calls among other things for the full protection of drivers against accidents. From work done by the Office of Science & Technology it is fairly clear that, while in the first phase benefits exceeded costs in that measurable accidents savings outweighed the costs imposed by extra regulations, in the second phase costs promise to out-weigh the benefits. While there is bound to be dispute about the valuations used there is little doubt about the very big difference in pay-offs between the two sets of legislation.

The fundamental point is – how much reduction in prospective damage shall we have? This is clearly illus-trated with pollution. Peter Walker in the first lecture received much support for his statement that the 'costs of removing the scars of pollution must be borne by those who create them' and for declaring also an individual firm's responsibility to be 'not to pollute'. But it is difficult to support both these ideas at once. The

absolute avoidance of pollution, which may be implied
by 'not to pollute', is an impossibly expensive rule for
society to adopt universally. On the other hand, we want
to do more, it seems, than what may be implied by the
first rule, namely to provide for restoration and compensation for pollution created by individual production
decisions taken without regard to pollution. Of course,
the important question is at what level of production of
the offensive output or outputs should one aim? In
principle, the answer is – at the level at which social costs
and benefits are balanced. The calculation of
advantage – the loss of output on the one hand, versus
the gain from reduced pollution on the other – must be
made. This is so whatever the means to be adopted to
secure the correct output levels.

But what means? Voluntary self-regulation? Government regulation? Or should one impose a tax or price on
output? Economists are fond of saying (I am myself) that
external costs such as pollution should be priced into
output so that costs fall on those who create them. An
inducement to avoid pollution is given, so that the
correct outputs will ensue. But airily suggesting that
pricing will solve the pollution problem (and thus will
reconcile growth and protection of the environment)
simply will not do. In fact the case for preferring taxing or
pricing to get the correct outputs, or, on the other hand,
regulating to get them, raises many complex issues of
which only a sketch can be given here. In principle,
regulation can secure the correct output to balance social
costs and benefits, as can pricing. But pricing has the
advantage, in principle, that it sets up a market. It allows
more easily for changing preferences for relief from the
damage caused to be expressed. This induces a useful

flexibility in response on the other side of the market. For example, in the case of one form of social cost — road congestion — one can in fact arrange for people to buy less congested running by charging vehicles by meters. The correct amount of compensation will vary greatly, by location, time or day, season, etc. Pricing can cope well with these variations. When variation is less, the advantage of pricing is less, *ceteris paribus.* But this kind of mechanism for pricing is much less easy to arrange in the case of pollution; so the practicability and cost of the mechanism has also to be considered. Again, prices or taxes imply revenues, regulation does not. Raising revenue, among other things, powerfully reinforces polluters' search to avoid pollution and gives them an incentive to monitor performance.

In selecting the instruments it is also important to consider costs of operation, and even more, their way of operating and the provision for change. Take regulation for example. It implies a continuing relationship between the regulators and the regulated. This helps the negotiation of standards of output acceptable and sensible from the industrial point of view and aids the spread of good practices in an affected industry. However, like dog-lovers and their dogs, the two parties — the regulators and the regulated — come to look remarkably like each other. Standards tend to become inflexible and the system rather impervious to outside influence. One of the areas in which we (and the rest of the world) have a long experience of regulation is transport. I think its history of resistance to changing social requirements is remarkable. It is almost impossible to conceive of regulatory bodies in transport, or for that matter other fields, which will advocate the substitution of different means of rationing output – especially radical ones. In short, without weighing the likely costs and benefits we cannot say which mode or instrument of policy will be preferable. Comparison of instruments is a sadly neglected area of study.[4] And in effect, I have argued that intervention is essentially a management problem for Government in selecting appropriate tools for policy.

There is no doubt, however, that whatever the degree of sophistication of calculation of benefit and loss, any system must rely on the voluntary compliance of companies and their management, following the lead given by law, custom and regulation, and the incentives of prices. Indeed the whole feasibility of a programme of social change depends on this, for there are strict limits to resources available to persuade citizens to move against their will. It is natural therefore to speculate about how education for management might or should be shaped to secure changing social ends, and I hope Philip Nind will take this up in the fourth lecture. Prospects and opportunities for change also much depend on developing technology, which creates opportunities for control as well as identifying many of the original problem areas. Lord Zuckerman will I hope address this during his talk.

Clearly, however, in an on-going system of redefining social aims, reviewing alternative means etc. in the way I have described, the feedback of new ideas is critical. Any approach to making social purposes effective must be prepared for change. At any time a new Carson or a new Nader may arise, and someone's computer is no doubt even now producing a new doomsday forecast. So that part of any system which deals with innovation in matters of social concern is very important indeed. I think business itself has an important role here, to which

I shall return. There I shall take up also the related question of what the individual firm should do to measure and communicate its own social performance, which is quite a topical, even fashionable question. First however, let me say something about the state of the art of measurement of social benefits and losses for use at the governmental decision-making level.

III Measurement of Social Benefits and Costs

We can conceive broadly of two kinds of measure of social benefits and costs, one for appraising total country performance and the other for application in individual parts of social and economic policy. The first might be used, for example, by governments and voters at general elections. What has been the country's total performance over time? How does it stand in the international league? Its use is essentially to bring pressure to bear for improvement via the political machinery. The second type of measurement is useful, as already indicated, for deciding particular courses of action. In an imperfect world, there is no necessary correspondence between the two, although one might hope for little conflict in practice. There is here some analogy with different measures of financial performance of companies: one needs an overall measure, even if rough, to chart a company's course over time; and some kind of project appraisal mechanism for an internal allocation of funds. One is provided by annual accounts, the other by a variety of specific measurement techniques.

Eli Goldston has proposed a measure of the first kind – 'A measurement of Economic Welfare' or 'MEW'.

The idea is to correct measure of gross national product, or total economy performance. First, one must deduct 'regrettables' – things one would rather do without, like defence expenditure and pollution. Then, one must add in such items as leisure time, housewives services, and do-it-yourself activity. The total is our 'MEW'. I must confess I see difficulties with it. Thus, if we note that last year there was an increase in a 'regrettable' – say more policemen – we cannot say whether this really *was* regrettable or on the contrary, was more than outweighed by feelings of extra security. To know this, we have to price the value of extra security against the cost of extra police. This perhaps could be done at the level of individuals in the society by observing personal trade-offs for security against expenditure; but one would be very wary of aggregating this to a national level. And the more one attempts to get value on *all* welfare items by adding individual measures, the more difficulty with aggregation is encountered.[5]

However, MEW is a useful corrective for cruder comparisons based on such restricted measures as GNP per head. As Eli Goldston showed us, the recent national record is far better in MEW than GNP terms. But we must be careful not to fall into the vulgar error of some politicians when they handle international league tables of GNP per head. What we should be interested in is absolute gains in welfare, and *not* so much worried about our relative standing among the nations.

When one considers the criteria for specific elements of social performance – pollution, amenity protection, accident prevention, and so forth, the trickiest problem is still to set a value on the outcome of policy. What is it worth to have pollution lessened, noise reduced etc?

Assuming one can predict who are affected, we would wish to set the benefits of reduction alongside costs, principally of reduced output, but also counting in the costs of alternative interventionary instruments.

Social cost benefit analysis (SCBA) has made some notable gains in the last ten years or so. For example, we can measure the benefits of road decongestion, some forms of air pollution and, thanks to the Roskill Commission on the third London Airport and the work inspired by it since, progress has been made in valuing noise nuisance.[6] But short of valuation in cost-benefit terms, one can use 'cost effective' comparisons. Here, essentially one sets up target levels of nuisances to be avoided or positive amenity to be achieved and compares costs of alternative means to reach the targets. If we have different target levels, and provided the costs of the means are well-behaved, we can set up quite elaborate potential trade-offs between possible expenditures and effects. These can then be submitted to policy-makers for choice. The advantage of actually attempting to value outcomes directly, as in SCBA, is that it promotes higher level rationality in allocation of resources — it provides, in principle, bridges between the different sectors of activity, for it values ends or objectives independently of the decision-making process. The snag of course is getting the values.

Recently much ingenuity has been displayed in setting up experimental conditions to infer values. For example, we have a 'Priority Evaluator' for environmental variables.[7] Here samples of people are asked to trade-off notional budgets (that is, allocate a store of points) between differing types of amenity, for example, de-creased journey to work, less noise, more safety, less

fumes, easier parking etc. Such experiments are beginning
to yield very interesting hypotheses about *relative* evaluation of these amenities. They lack, however, a connection
to the real world of sacrifices and actual money expenditure. The most acceptable valuations to those actually
deciding on where to invest, subsidise, or whatever, have
so far proved to be rooted in observations of people's
actual behaviour in trading off money against an attribute
of value to them. An outstanding example, the valuation
of time spent travelling, is now quite widely accepted as a
guide in deciding the value of alternative actions to lessen
urban congestion. Progress in valuing many items of
amenity, or its converse, nuisance, (e.g. in pollution and
noise) has also depended on extracting the value of
attributes revealed in property transactions, thus again
appealing to observed behaviour, this time in actual
markets. But here especially we encounter the full
barrage of objections to such endeavours.

Objections come from many quarters. Welfare economists can see snags in assuming that the values derived
from property transactions actually match what it is
desired to measure. In the case of, say, a prospective
increase in airport noise, we want to know the amount
needed to compensate those affected and leave them no
worse off. But in appealing to market behaviour can one
allow for the income effects of a change properly? What
about the balance of supply and demand for houses
offering differing amenity levels? Can one control
properly in one's measures for this? These and many
more objections are essentially criticisms of method,
which in principle are open to improvement.[8] Many
people simply object on the grounds that it is somehow
immoral to attempt to set a cash value, or equivalent to a

cash value, on such items as human life (as in accident prevention cost-benefit analysis), on a Norman church, or on a species of fish in a threatened ecological chain. To some extent this is just sloppy thinking. Actually of course we implicitly value all these things when we refuse to increase the budgets we are prepared to spend to promote such ends. But the objections are based on more than sentiment, I think. Probably the feeling is that it is wrong to let professionals, and economists in particular, to appear to pre-empt, or worse, *actually* to pre-empt, decisions by applying the results of what seem to be dubious and mysterious calculations. To some extent, again, this is the kind of difficulty that any new method or analysis encounters in being adopted in a decision-making system or organisation. Enthusiasts exaggerate their claims for a new technique, opponents predict dire outcomes from adopting it. The real problem is deciding on the way in which decisions are to be made. No one really supposes that important, complex decisions would ever be made in measured cost benefit items alone even if measured satisfactorily; SCBA, like other decision-making techniques, *aids* decisions.

There is really little danger, I feel, from *attempts* at SCBA evaluation. The technical or experimental difficulties of getting suitable measurement conditions will always, in my view, limit its use: I cannot easily forsee a time, for example, when we will be able satisfactorily to measure (by reference to actual choices) the value of saving lives. True, one *can* see possibilities in devising schemes to test the value an individual sets on his own life; but there are more difficulties if we ask the additional relevant question — what is the value we set on each other's lives? Nevertheless, because we vote with budget allocations for old people's medicine, on the one hand, and prevention of infectious children's diseases on the other, we have a *moral* obligation to face up to the question of values. The attempt to measure is surely right. Looking at what we have done with our budget allocations in the past does not give the answer, because we presumably wish to challenge the relative sizes of the budgets.

But the spirit of enquiry and challenge inevitably accompanying attempts to set values on desired objectives does raise problems of organising decision-making. Such problems, I believe, arose with Roskill. This was a great attempt at rational evaluation in public; but its own mechanics and terms of reference prevented much practical use being made of the controversy its cost benefit analysis aroused. Specifically, there was little feed-back from its analysis to the possibility of selecting other, and perhaps better sites than the four considered; or indeed to the possibility of deciding that no site at all was required. And the heat generated by the form of enquiry made it that much more difficult for the normal political process which Roskill served to avoid choosing one of the four.

More progress with SCBA can perhaps be made where controversy is less immediately in the public eye. In the context of the urban environment, our work on the Urban Motorways Committee, for example, allowed plenty of debate. We were able to consider the extension of Roskill's work on aircraft noise to the more important area, in the aggregate, of road vehicle noise. SCBA work on this area requires a most complicated piece of modelling. Essentially, one confronts distributions of values housholders set on noise avoidance with distributions of values the same set puts on staying where they are (called 'householders surplus'). One then posits an increase in noise nuisance from traffic. Where noise value is predicted to outweigh values of staying, a household moves; where the reverse is true, it stays put and grins and bears it. Different net costs to households emerge, according to these effects. Now, on the Committee we debated a great deal about the legitimacy of these costs and the methods used and were able to give a cautious blessing to developing them further. But the important thing was that the Committee accepted the legitimacy of the concept of loss of householders' surplus. This rechristened as 'home loss', found its way into the Bill mentioned earlier.[9]

Several other significant things emerged from the Committee's deliberations. First, we found it more useful to think of SCBA as a planning tool rather than an *exact* basis for assessing compensation to those affected. Valuation is more feasible for groups than for individuals. This was because one could more plausibly predict the effects over total populations than for individuals. So we were led to stress the adaptations of the planning processes which could capitalise on this sort of information, by, for example, choosing among several ways of noise prevention and taking account of users' losses and gains. Second, careful attention to *who* would be affected, to what extent, and how this might vary in different situations was reinforced. We came out of our three years work much clearer than before about the extent and incidence of noise nuisance. For example, we sharpened our appreciation that the pattern would be a few badly affected, and many rather little affected.[10] Our consultants were able to establish much more firmly the relations between effects on numbers of people, and the costs of avoidance of noise, by differing means. We could set these numbers alongside number and cost avoidance estimates of other disamentities, notably severance, which as I said earlier, turned out to be a rather more serious problem than we had imagined at the beginning. So in this case perhaps the most solid technical gains were, in fact, extending the basis for cost-effective actions.

The return to more work in the field of cost effectiveness indeed seems to be high, and every month brings new examples, especially in the field of pollution.[11] But if I had to choose an area in which it seems to me the pay-off is now the highest, it would be accident prevention. There is no doubt that, taking a criterion like "maximise the avoidance of deaths per £ spent', we are illogical about the relative effort devoted to say, air, road, rail and and industrial safety, to say nothing of preventive medicine. The implicit valuation of life in those spheres varies enormously. The criterion to be followed can be argued endlessly. For example, I can hear my fellow professionals asking questions like 'what is the rate of substitution of serious injuries for deaths avoided?' But the criterion has good egalitarian appeal as a working tool. The point is that we can hardly go wrong in working *towards* equalising the implied value of life. If this criterion *were* taken seriously at the appropriate level, all sorts of interesting analyses could be pulled together. For example, we would consider carefully the different phases of accidents — before, during and after. Is it more cost-effective to go in for prophylaxis (safety training); or for improvement of conditions at the potential accident site; or for getting help to the injured quickly? Which organisations actually now have the smallest implied value of life, and which the highest? (In transport, for example, railways probably have the highest.) What is involved in shifting resources among the several uses? I suspect the main difficulty in achieving improvement will be organisational, leading to the need to answer such questions as where is the pay-off to the initiator of improvements, what change in bureaucratic boundaries will be needed, and what resistance encountered?

This raises again the problem of generating the candidates for social treatment. I often feel that, in my sphere of environmental competence, transport, the most important result of SCBA analysis so far has in fact been the gradually growing influence which analysis has had on project generation. There is a good deal more variety and subtlety nowadays in propositions for urban improvement. There is also a serious question of the pay-offs to research and development to environmental issues. Some ecological chains are, as we know, very long and effects very remote. How do we know which to investigate and how far do we pursue them? Now I hope Lord Zuckerman will throw light on this in his lecture, but from the discussion so far it seems that at an early stage such work should have some regard to likely cost-effective pay-offs. It should look forward to at least the main modes of control or influence, and should have a capacity to generate further cost-effective questions. To some extent, this is a question of education, for scientists, civil servants and management; and so our discussion of the fourth lecture in the series will have much relevance to this topic also.

IV   Measurement of Company Social Performance

Now let me turn to what the 'socially responsible'
company might do to measure its own activities (I will
come back to the question of how far it *should* be
responsible and so go in, if rational, for measuring its
social performance in a final section.)

It has become fashionable to talk of a 'Corporate
Social Audit',[1][2] in principle designed to measure the
impact of the company on the society in which it works.
Clearly, the prospects for realistic measurement in terms
of value or cost are in general less good for companies
than they are for governments – the job of disentangling
suitably disaggregated figures is even more formidable.
Also there are certainly returns to scale in investigatory
effort – the government may get more return from its
research £ in this area than private firms do. But this in
effect is to look at any given company as facing a sample
drawn at random from the social issues exercising the
nation. Sometimes this is inappropriate. Specifically,
where a company's activity forms an appreciable part of
a local economy – as for large plants in isolated areas –
then the principal social issue is that of the impact on the
local economy from investment or disinvestment, notably
the induced-effects on local incomes. Here it is possible
to measure a total impact, and indeed aids to this (for
example calculations of local or regional income multi-
pliers) are burgeoning.

But for the general run of companies is it sensible to
attempt any general 'correction' of a company's reported
results to reflect its social performance? Flirting with
temptation, could one apply Eli Goldston's notions of
MEW at national level to individual company sales and

outlay data or gross product? Thus might one deduct 'regrettables' (e.g. expenditure on work's police) and add leisure time, perhaps. Economists, warming up to the exercise, would want to correct inputs used by a company for their shadow prices – e.g. labour employed at the price reflecting the local employment situation. Exports might be revalued at the shadow price of foreign exchange. Getting still more enthusiastic, let's revalue output at prices discounting monopoly power, if any, and add in (deduct?) a proper opportunity cost of the chairman and his board.

The basic trouble about these is not so much that they raise the spectre of unfair comparisons – there is plenty of unfairness about financial comparisons – it is that they do not measure anything useful to guiding company choices in action to pursue social ends. For this, as we have seen, two conditions are necessary, a feedback of prospective impact to prospective actions, and a valuation of the impacts. For this specific cost benefit work is again necessary in which each company will decide for itself the social weights to be assigned to its analyses.

Then what about, as has been suggested, polling the public to show how different companies rate for their good social orientation? This could be more or less sophisticated. The less sophisticated version is easily refutable. Simple opinion polling tends to reflect companies' latest expenditure on attractive advertising. Consumers can easily be revealed inconsistent between actual voting (the cash they pay to a company) and reporting their opinions (their ranking of companies).

But again warming to the task, more sophisticated experiments could be devised. For example, to borrow from marketing one might speculate about the use of non-metric scaling of social preferences for companies. The procedure might be to ask respondents simply to think of the general beneficial social impact of each company in a set of companies. One would ask the respondents to rank pairs of companies in terms of their similarity. From this information one might derive social dimensions which are consistent with those that must have been in respondents' minds when they ranked the pairs of companies. The next step is to label the dimensions. One might, for example, be company attitudes in labour relations. Thus one could gauge how individual companies rate on these dimensions. The information could be used to guide the choice of company to invest in; and a company itself might measure its own divergence from average social performance of companies in its industry or sector. It would be interesting to put nationalised industries in the sample, too. Needless to say, we need careful selections of the respondent populations for valid results!

V The Practice of Social Concern

The ordinary social responsible company will probably forgo what it would regard flights of fancy like this. Very likely it will go through a sober process of defining specific social goals, defining means, securing resources, providing for feed-back etc. And it will do something like Eastern Gas & Fuel Associates, and simply establish separate budgets devoted to its social concerns, alongside the normal financial one, for example a community budget and a charity budget. By reviewing progress against budgets it will over time build up to a series of cost-effective exercises for social objectives. It will have to agonise about the implicit trade-offs among budgets, and it would no doubt find that pressures to reallocate them will vary according to who is admitted to the voting (political) system of the company. Should a company be obliged to explain and justify to shareholders and public its social expenditures? This is difficult to answer. Often a company will wish to explain its actions; but I am doubtful about compelling detailed disclosure. Though to digress a moment, I think that there is merit in compelling further disclosure of financial transactions with the objective of enabling the capital markets in particular to do their work of allocation better, this is always purchased at a risk of specific commercial disadvantage, and itself requires a nice exercise in cost benefit analysis by the state. It would be perhaps unwise to impose further obligations which might have the incidental effect of abnormal commercial disclosure. And it is inherently much more difficult to establish standards here than for ordinary financial transactions.

This brings me, developing points put by Peter Walker, to the question of what should be the relative roles of the Government, industry collectively and the individual company in social responsibility? From what I have said, you will not be surprised to hear that my bias is towards emphasising the government's responsibilities for social decision-making (I include local in the term government here). If the common aims of securing growth and desirable social ends are to be sensibly maintained, a rigorous well-thought-out and quantified framework is essential. Otherwise those trade-offs by default between growth and social objectives that I mentioned earlier will not diminish. The prime responsibility for setting this up is a Government. The Government (or a large local government) alone is likely to have the technical competence to investigate the value of social action or its cost effectiveness. It must take responsibility for deciding between instruments of policy, which I have argued are an essential part of its analysis.

Let us take the duties that Peter Walker assigned in his lecture to industry as opposed to the tasks he assigns to the Government. First his view that 'Industry should not pollute.' Yes, agreed given that edict comes from the Government's analysis and the analysis indicates production to give zero pollution. He thinks companies have responsibilities to support regional policy and labour retraining. I am happy with this so long as it is clear that the Government sets the framework and, for example, gives the subsidies which it deems appropriate, given its beliefs about company reaction. Most of the rest of his desiderata for companies I think can be left to enlightened self-interest (including profit-sharing, job enlargement and the development of employees' self-realisation).

As a mediator between companies (and other interests) and the state, organised industry has I think responsibility for helping along the ends clearly enunciated by the Government, by attempting to persuade member firms to improve standards etc. This again is realisable in terms of enlightened self-interest. Organised interests are in a bargaining position with the state; they must give service having the effect of furthering state ends, or lowering state costs, for concessions to their own economic interests.

But should the individual company nevertheless pursue a social strategy of its own? The most powerful business

school advocate for this has perhaps been Harvard's
Ken Andrews.[1][3] He argues roughly as follows. A company should have a positive strategy for social responsibility. It should incorporate this in normal corporate
planning processes. A portfolio of socially acceptable
projects should be developed so that a company among
other things can withdraw from projects which prove to
be socially unacceptable (if one's best investment turns
out to support Black African repression, for example).
Further, on analysis it may well turn out anyway that
there is *no* conflict between the social and private aims of
a project. Thus pollution avoidance by investment in its
suppression may sometimes turn out to give valuable
by-products of greater value than the extra investment
cost. So far so good.

But then, suppose there really is a difficult problem in
that competitors will not follow socially desirable expenditures? Also, perhaps consumerism is *too* vigilant in the
industry's sector to allow these to be made. 'Don't
worry,' he says, in effect, Big business calls the tune.
And, he argues, business needs to be socially responsible
to be able to hire good young managers (probably very
true). But at the end of the day, one might well ask, what
guarantees consensus and therefore compatability of
social aims with competitive vigour? His answer seems to
be by developing a professional ethic. The profession of
management will – and must, he argues, – develop
agreed social aims. Business practice follows and all is
well.

Now one does not have to be a follower of Milton
Friedman and the Chicago School to part company with
Andrews at this point. The objection is a simple one. One
cannot rely upon a profession, however will-intentioned,

to be responsive to ever-changing social needs. That is the function, in a democracy, of persuading the government, and it seems to me that reform of state institutions is a far better way of improving society's responsiveness. (It is hard enough already to express my and your private judgements through the ballot box in systems set up for that purpose.) What we should be thinking about, rather, is new ways in which all persons' preferences can be expressed. Development of measurements in the way I have discussed is one important way; and there are many other possibilities of achieving a more responsive state. So I reject the 'professional' part of the Andrews model.

It follows that I am all for diversity of social ends in business, consistent with the framework established by the Government. By all means let companies compete along social lines. I set considerable store by that underrated side of company innovation, the eccentric social experiment. Let consumerism or any other reform aimed at fostering growth keep up market place pressure, but if a business can make the profits, let it 'waste' them (according to *my* tastes) on 'useless' social projects. What *I* think appropriate or inappropriate now may well be the guiding light of government planners fifteen years from now. Remember how Cadbury's experiments in housing in the nineteenth century became a model to inspire town planners of the 1950s. The state should be very selective in responding to calls to intervene for social ends, and it is greatly helped in its task by a wide generation of possible lines of social advance.

Finally let me say positively what I think is the *prime* social responsibility of business. Social responsibility is fundamentally caring for others, but caring actively, that is by supplying what one has in abundance to others. If one looks at the great estates of the realm and asks, what can each give to enrich the others, one is bound to say of the private enterprise sector that its relative advantage, its most valuable resource, is in the skills of management, thus in translating ideals into effective action. This is not to deny that there has been in the past a drain of talent to other estates of the realm; indeed this is one of the reasons now underlying the high opportunity cost of managerial ability in social terms. Business's chief social responsibility is to give of its skills. I welcome moves voluntarily to extend executives' time to service of the community. And, we have to take far more seriously the question of how do we divert more talent to the approved social ends of governments? Some of this diversion will come, I am sure, with greater executive choice and leisure and the private enterprise trend of social experimentation of which I have spoken. But this will not be enough, probably. The Government could well take measures to increase companies' willingness to take part in social experiments — whether on their own initiative or in concert with central or local government — for example by fiscal means. The cost in normal commercial terms to a company in lending good executives' time is not the salary itself so much as the loss of earning power to the company. We should be able to devise tax allowances which properly reflect this sacrifice. (If this is done, disclosure of activities is of course necessary.)

Now, in another great estate, the Civil Service, we have probably the largest existing body of would-be social innovators. As those who have served in it will know, schemes for social improvement abound there as nowhere else. If my analysis is right, the pay-off to a larger exchange between the 'estates' will be high; each side gaining to its great advantage. True, this has been already done, but, in relation to needs, only on a lamentably small scale. Perhaps again this is fundamentally an educational problem, of training men and women to be capable of moving between the 'estates' and to be more valuable to each. If we are to have more effective exchanges, then this will only come if the needs, first, are analysed similarly. The Stockton Lectures are meant to help in hammering out such a consensus.

But we need to give the exchanges other encouragement. As companies become more aware of social responsibilities, I expect an increasing recuitment of able people from the Civil Service to industry, and earlier in their careers than this usually happens now. If, as I would hope, secondments from the Civil Service to industry become part of civil servants' training programmes, this would encourage the process. The greater difficulty is arranging a reciprocal exposure in the young business executives' training. Once these young executives can see career advantages and advancement in industry from experience in the social sector the personal motivation will be there. To set the good precedents, however, requires far-seeing industrial leadership. I conclude with one idea which might help: there is a perpetual problem in the public sector of actually getting 'think-tanks' to put concentrated study into long-term developments of social policy. The immediate always intrudes. Consultants hired from outside in the normal commercial way have their limitations. Why not then encourage the *internal* consultancy services in which many large firms now concentrate some of their best young brains to take on some public sector assignments? Perhaps it is already done; perhaps it has difficulties. But it could be a substantial contribution to the exchange I wish to see greatly developed. We will all have different views on this, I suspect, but if one outcome of the Stockton Lectures is a fresh look at interaction between industry and the Civil Service, I will be very content.

NOTES

1 'Probabilities of a World Energy Crisis', *National Westminster Bank Quarterly Review*, Nov. 1972.
2 A Bill now before Parliament gives the right for compensation when public works adversely affect property values but do not require the property, or part of it, for the works.
3 The Report of the Committee was dated July 1972. Department of the Environment: 'New Roads in Towns': Report of the Urban Motorways Committee (Chairman: W. Burns), 56pp.
4 This comment particularly applies to pricing or taxing. As methods of control these are flexible, but need a great deal of effort in monitoring. I have discussed some of the problems in the field of congestion pricing for roads in my book, *Urban Transport. Studies in Economic Policy*, Butterworth 1973, especially Chapter 9. Banning, or requiring zero output, is the least flexible (and is intended to be). Presumably the decision is that it is unlikely that any change in social requirements will require positive output. Banning is usually a low cost form of control requiring only 'policing.' But there is still a question of how the case for change of a ban gets

channelled and acted upon.

5 All successful cost benefit work (for this is what this is) requires good conditions for what is known to economists as 'partial equilibrium analysis', i.e. an unchanging background against which to measure differences denoting the presence of a cost or a benefit. National figures do not easily provide this, unfortunately.

6 Commission on the Third London Airport (Chairman: The Hon. Mr. Justice Roskill): Report, HMSO, London 1971. See especially Chapter 7.

7 Described in A. Lassiere and P. Bowers, 'Studies in the Social Costs of Urban Road Transport (Noise and Pollution) 18th Round Table', European Conference of Ministers of Transport, April 1972.

8 What a pity it is still so difficult, in this connection, for research workers to use that immensely rich source of data on property transactions stored up in the Inland Revenue since before the War.

9 See footnote 2.

10 To make a personal observation, not that of the Committee, this kind of information is critical to the selection of instruments of policy. Highly concentrated effects point to action specific to the location rather than to the originators of the noise, the vehicles. Thus, *cet. par.,* a change in expectation of incidence of nuisance like this will incline one more to physical action (on roads for example) rather than a noise tax on vehicles in general; or to a site-specific noise tax or price rather than a requirement to substitute quieter engines. (Needless to say *'cet. par.'* is important.)

11 In the Autumn 1972 issue of *Quarterly Review of*

Economics and Business, in 'Costs of Air Pollution Control in the Coal-fired Electric Power Industry', W.D. Watson examined alternative costs of pollution in the coal-fired electric power industry, following the quality standard set in the US by the Clean Air Amendments of 1970, and in the context of an expected four-fold increase in coal firing for electric plants in the US up to 2000. The principal options to reach the standards are to invest in sulphur dioxide removal or to substitute low sulphur coal, and with either, to combine with fly ash removal plant. Most variations in cost arise from the location of coal resources of differing qualities and the associated transport and pollution removal costs. Thus for a new Minneapolis coal-fired plant a low cost pollution strategy is found to be burning low sulphur Wyoming coal rather than Illinois or Kentucky coal. Interesting incidental points emerge. Strip mining of coal is assumed, where costs are lower. This may raise other environmental questions. Current technique – total desulphurisation before combustion – is rejected as being less effective in removing sulphur than an alternative process, limestone injection with wet scrubbing, because it allows only small reductions in sulphur, but is up to four times as cheap a process. So the standard adopted disallows what might be 'better' solutions for some conditions and locations.

Robert E. Kohn, in the *Review of Economics and Statistics,* Nov. 1972 'Price Elasticities of Demand and Air Pollution Control' added to his earlier work on cost-effective means of dealing with 94 'pollution source categories' in the St. Louis airshed. He concluded that, allowing for reactions of demand for products affected by necessary taxes to achieve pollution standards, the cost of reaching the standards would be $34.9 million. The main changes implied for consumption would be for example much greater for gasoline than for coal-fired plants.

12 Compare R.A. Bauer and D.H. Fenn, 'What is a Corporate Social Audit?' *Harvard Business Review*, Jan/Feb. 1973.

13 In K.R. Andrews, *The Concept of Corporate Strategy*, Dow Jones-Irwin, 1971.

FOUR

Technological Development
and its Application

S. ZUCKERMAN

The theme to which I have been asked to address myself is the role of technology in serving the social purposes which were outlined in the first two of these Stockton Lectures. The objectives which they laid before us were nothing if not far-reaching. To summarise Mr. Peter Walker's message in a few words: he was advocating the elimination of poverty; the improvement of the relations of employer to employee through closer participation in the discharge of their respective responsibilities for the economic well-being of the country; the prevention of the degradation of the physical environment in which we live and work; and, in general, the improvement of what is loosely called these days 'the quality of life'. Professor Beesley endorsed these goals, but focused our attention mainly on 'problems of social concern', and on the need to use techniques of social benefit/cost analysis in deciding how to achieve the right social ends.

A cynic might well say that I have been given an impossible task, and that what I have been asked to do in the space of some forty-five minutes is to show how technology can bring peace, prosperity and goodwill to all men and not only to the men of today but also to those of tomorrow. The issues, however, are not those which should inspire cynicism. Although I obviously am not in the course of a lecture going to try to provide a blueprint which delineates the future role of technology – even were this within my capacity – I shall not therefore shrink from my general remit.

My first reason for being so brash is that it is precisely the improvement of man's lot that has been a main spur to technology since the dawn of civilisation. If this had not been the case, or had not been thought to be the case, the technological developments which have both enlarged and constrained the horizons within which we live would surely have been suppressed, and not encouraged. We constantly need to remind ourselves that technology has always been with us, and that it has always been an immensely important determinant of the social, economic, and political framework within which all men exist, regardless of differences in their ways of life. For what we mean by technology is simply the organised exploitation of available scientific knowledge in order to provide people with the things they need or want, or are persuaded they want, and for which they yearn as they strive for an ever better material life. Primitive or pre-scientific technology provided the first framework for settled village life. A more advanced technology made urban life possible. An even more advanced technology underlies our own highly industrialised civilisation. In short, the culture of society always reflects its technology, and the fruits of technology continually transform society. If some kinds of technology now threaten man's well-being, it is man's own fault for having encouraged the wrong technology.

My task, however, has not been simplified by Professor Beesley's *a priori* acceptance of current 'social concerns' as goals which one accepts *a priori*, even though he admits that it is a fascinating question how particular issues like pollution, conservation, noise avoidance, job rewards, visual amenity, or safety, became established as social ends. He himself did not try to answer this question which, however, is critical to the task that has been set me in this lecture. For to my way of thinking, technology, which continually interacts with new scientific knowledge, is far more than a means whereby human aspirations are satisfied. It has always been, and it remains, a critical determinant in the emergence of our social values. The industrial revolution had its origins in Western Europe, and for the most part in the United Kingdom, but its spread was seldom impeded in the same way as the values it generates go on being encouraged the whole world over. There have, of course, always been a few vocal sects or groups within industrialised societies which have yearned for what they believe is a different, a simpler, and a wiser life. And there have also been a few primitive communities, like the food-gathering Bushmen of the Kalahari, which have refused to be drawn into the net of modern society. But the overwhelming majority of mankind is not like this.

We live as we live today because of the decisions, however explicit or however undefined, that were taken yesterday about which technological developments to encourage in satisfying man's enduring urge for an even better life — for a life from which the fear of starvation and sudden death have been eliminated, and for a life in which health is assured and the burden of labour lightened. The world has become richer and healthier through technology, and the fact that it has not at the same time become more peaceful, or a world in which there are no poor, is not the fault of technologists. It is surely unnecessary to say that there are other forces which shape man's social and political destiny.

Be that as it may, technology is as potent a factor as any in the process whereby, in that apt phrase, we get 'painted into a corner'. The internal combustion engine and motor car, the telephone, radio and television, DDT, modern techniques of sanitation, food preservatives, refrigerators, and electric power, are only a minute sample of the technical and essential fabric of modern civilisation, and in particular of urban civilisation. Without electric power an ever-increasing proportion of the urban population of industrialised societies would become prisoners in their high-tower buildings. Without chemicals to preserve the food transported to them from the countryside and from abroad, they would starve. We know what happens when the railways do not run, or when electric power and gas are cut off. A vast and growing proportion of the world's population is urbanised. Our own population is already entirely dependent on the industrial civilisation which started less than three hundred years ago, and it requires no long memory to realise what the essential services provided by modern technology mean to the maintenance of our way of life. The same is true of every industrialised country, and it is equally true of countries which are now struggling to better their lots through industrialisation, through the modernisation of agriculture, through better education, and through modern social services, including modern medicine. It is only recently that we read harrowing stories of emaciated peasant farmers moving with their starved cattle from their parched fields into the city of Bombay, hoping to find there the water of which drought has deprived them. But in what direction would the inhabitants of our cities flee? Certainly not to the country! There they would starve. Half the food we now consume in the United Kingdom is grown on the prairies or fields of other countries. In short, we are now locked into our technological past, and are impelled to the future by the hope of still more and still better technology. We cannot turn back, because there is no 'back' to which to turn.

In our own country, in the USA and USSR, in Japan, and to varying degrees in other countries, there is, however, concern that the growth of population, associated with rising standards of living deriving from the spread of industry, as well as from modern techniques of food production, are endangering the future of our species because of the pollution and devastation of our physical environment, and because of the possible exhaustion of the raw materials on which an industrial civilisation depends. Fears are also drummed into us that not only are our amenities under constant threat, but that we are being poisoned by dangerous chemicals emitted into the atmosphere, or poured into our rivers, or incorporated into our food. There is also the well-known fact that the growth and spread of human population is associated with a reciprocal threat to the remaining wild fauna and flora of the world. As our demands increase, as forests are felled and new land brought into use in underdeveloped parts of the world, the existing flora and fauna suffer. The effort to stem this process, or at least to protect living species other than man, is at the root of the conservation movement. And this began decades ago, long before our present concern with environmental pollution and the exhaustion of our physical resources.

A 'package message' of doom has recently been provided in that widely publicised emanation of Dr. D. Meadows, formerly of the Massachusetts Institute of Technology, but, contrary to common belief, not published under the *imprimatur* of that famous institution, but under the auspices of a so-called 'secret college', the Club of Rome, under the title *The Limits of Growth*.[1] The theme of this book is that unless we mend our ways; unless we bring about an abrupt change in our industrial processes and in our patterns of consumption; and unless we stop breeding at more than replacement rate, our society will come to a grinding halt in a minute fraction of the time that it has taken to evolve. This is what is now envisaged as the 'Predicament of Man'.

I am no computer expert, and in this lecture I am not going to add to the chorus of criticism which has greeted Dr. Meadows' publication. I have done so in a modest way elsewhere.[2] But for the purposes of my address today it is necessary to say that I reject his conclusions because they add up to a message of hopelessness. For all its pseudo-scientific and computerised look, the bulk of what Meadows has provided us is a tangle of tautologies. What is true in his message is not new, and what is new is not necessarily true. One reason for the unsophisticated superficiality of the book is that while it talks about the exponential growth of population, pollution, and the use of resources, it avoids any proper mention of the exponential growth of human knowledge, and of the increase in the kind of understanding with which we can imbue our efforts as we see to it that our increasing numbers do not become incompatible with a better life, and with a physical environment which is not just a reflection of what the doomwatchers deplore in what they see around them now. The computerised world in which Meadows weaves his fancies is devoid of real people, and unruffled by 'social feed-backs'.

I regard the book as one of the more recent manifestations of a phase of despair through which the world, or our part of it, is passing, and one which is associated with other signs of anti-intellectualism, and in particular of a disillusionment with science and technology. On the basis of our knowledge of similar phases, we could regard the present one as unimportant, were it not for the fact that powerful and rapid social changes are afoot in almost every advanced country, and that the urge for higher standards of living generally, and for a more equitable sharing of wealth than characterises the present, are accelerating the normal rate of growth in the demand for goods and services. In particular, those vast areas of the globe which house the bulk of the world's population are in turmoil as their inhabitants try to improve their lot in every way that seems at hand — whether it be through industry, or agriculture, or mining — or through expropriation.

The whole world is convulsed by change. The oppressed millions will not remain down-trodden; and not surprisingly the rich do not themselves want to become poor as wealth is redistributed. 'No growth in a stationary state' is not a slogan for the masses — whatever its meaning may be to certain way-out environmentalists and self-appointed ecologists — for the world's deprived population is not going to desist in its efforts to lift itself from the dust while others speculate about the cost of their doing so. The world is in a hurry, and we cannot afford the inaction brought about by the unnecessarily generated despair of pseudo-scientific soothsayers. Because of increased literacy, and because we now have the radio and television, the power of the word has never been stronger than it is today. A few Western eyes and ears may have seen and heard and may even believe the message that all is already lost. But in underprivileged parts of the world, there is a clarion call to a battle to capture the trappings of Western civilisation while there is still time, in spite of the fact that the battle is one for which they may be ill-prepared by education. Some of the 'values' which the Meadows message calls forth in the Western world, the values to which Professor Beesley referred in his lecture, have all but no relevance to those vast areas of the globe whose population outnumbers that of the industrial West, but with whose fate our own is inextricably linked. And with economic growth a natural goal everywhere, the doom message cannot but help to get world priorities about values wrong.

I shall return to this question later. But first let me say where technology is not going to help in implementing the values which Mr. Walker and Professor Beesley laid before us. To start with, technology is not going to produce peace on earth, nor is it going to succeed – where the Church has so far failed – in making us heed the injunction 'Love thy neighbour as thyself.' Second, while technology may be essential for the elimination of poverty, its role in this respect is secondary to politics. Third, while technology helps provide the means whereby the rate of population growth could be slowed down, it cannot be held responsible if the rate does not go down, or even if it goes up. Fourth, technology might help improve employer/employee relationships, but only on the condition that both sides of industry – and there are still two sides, whether in socialist or capitalist societies — agree about the balance between productivity and output in relation to capital on the one hand, and opportunities for employment on the other. Automating plants reduces the demand for labour, and shutting them down in order to achieve a more economic use of resources is no less an unpopular measure today than it was a hundred or two hundred years ago. We are all Luddites in our resistance to change.

Above all technology — whether the technology of the pre-computer, computer, or conceivably post-computer age — is not going to dictate the social values which should guide our steps. It transforms the social environment within which our values are formed, but before the environment becomes changed, technology cannot say what new or altered values are likely to emerge. Did anyone in Mr. Henry Ford's workshops know how his inventions were going to transform our way of life? How they were going to generate seemingly endless and insuperable problems? What about the products of Mr. Thomas Edison's workshop — leave alone those of IBM today? What about Whittle's jet engine or Watson Watt's radar?

Let me turn now to those aspirations which technology does and can continue to help to make a reality. As they always have, these values relate to that vast spectrum of activities which directly improve our physical well-being, our standards of health and nutrition, and our prosperity. Today they also relate to measures designed to improve the physical environment in which we live — measures which reduce the pollution of our rivers, the levels of noise to which we are subjected, traffic congestion and so on. No one wishes to live a short and brutish life if he can avoid doing so. But again, who determines our material social values? The answer is that since they reflect the innate desires of the vast majority of mankind, we have to assume that they are arrived at democratically, and that they will be attended to in a rational order of priority. The harbingers of doom, and the minority groups of a new breed of environmentalists, seem to disregard this elemental truth of society. It is surely not for them to decide whether steps to reduce levels of noise, or measures to cause a fractional decrease in SO_2 in the air, or to remove some food preservative from consumption should come before new housing or more schools and hospitals, or better pensions for the aged.

One prerequisite for the timely development of useful technology is that informed scientists themselves speak up on these matters, and that they do not leave the task entirely to professional journalists. The public is daily regaled with tales of the extraordinary, or of new, horrors purported to stem from new scientific technological developments. In fact only a handful of scientists are speaking up today, and unfortunately some of them have also discovered that it is easier and more profitable to write about sensational disbenefits than about the multitudinous benefits which science and technology have brought and can bring to man.

The Americans have a strict law to ensure that the food they eat is 'pure' and that the drugs they take are not harmful. One of its many amendments is named after a Congressman, Mr. Delaney, and in effect it lays down that no substance can be licensed for public consumption if any quantity of it can be shown to be carcinogenic in man or experimental animals. During the past few years, the American public have become acutely aware of this amendment. So too, in greater measure, have the American food and drug industry and the pharmacological departments in universities. It is said that the 'pill', which passed through the licensing sieve some years ago, and whose potential for good in preventing unwanted pregnacies is enormous, would almost certainly have been prohibited today, since its main constituents can, in certain circumstances, be shown to be carcinogenic in test animals. With the increasing sensitivity of measuring instruments, instruments which can detect chemicals in parts per thousand million, we can expect that ever-increasing numbers of chemical agents which in absolute terms may be carcinogenic, but which in a practical sense are harmless, will be identified. Some natural foods which have been part of normal diets for hundreds of years could be trapped in the net of the Delaney Amendment because of the chemicals with which they have been endowed by Nature. One effect of this heightening of concern for presumed safety is that it deters the search for new drugs to alleviate pain and sickness.

Scientists cannot prove a negative. It is one of the responsibilities of the U.S. National Academy of Sciences to help the US Food and Drug Administration (the 'FDA') on these matters. Two years ago, they had to advise that, when given in large quantities, a food additive in common use produced bladder tumours in a small number of experimental rats. The facts were plain in the test protocols that were examined, and once this was so, the Academy could make no further comment. The chemical substance in question then had to be proscribed by the FDA. It was not the Academy's business to give a view about the relationship of the risks involved to the social benefits which from that moment on were going to be denied, any more than the Academy had been called upon to advise about the particular piece of legislation concerned. What is more, if they had been asked the blunt but misleading question, should substances which can be shown to be carcinogenic be included in food-stuffs, there was only one answer they could have given — No. And no other answer could be given by any responsible body or person. That was in fact the answer which the New York Academy of Sciences gave in a very recent comment on the Delaney Amendment.

But the question the Delaney Amendment poses is totally unscientific. There are risks in everything we do. What needs to be considered is not absolute, but relative risk. Our own legislation once decreed that the domestic consumer should be provided with 'pure and wholesome' water. In due course we dropped the word 'pure' — because it is impossible to define scientifically what 'pure water' is, unless it be distilled water.

The average expectation of life of the British popula-tion has now risen to practically asymptotic levels in all age groups, and the health of the community goes on improving. Yet we are being constantly warned about the dangers of sulphur dioxide in the atmosphere, about the risk of poisoning by the carbon monoxide and lead emitted by cars, or by mercury and cadmium in our rivers and estuaries, and by a host of other toxic substances. But on few, if any, of these matters is there any scientific consensus about what constitutes acceptable risk and about what levels of what substances in our environment are significantly injurious to health. If we wish to put our problems of social concern — to use Professor Beesley's term — into reasonable perspective, the first thing that is needed is that responsible scientists should get together, both nationally and internationally, to agree rational toxicity standards. We cannot afford, nor do we want, absolute standards. Because conditions differ, we also do not need uniform standards. What we want are flexible standards which relate to particular circumstances and which can be changed as knowledge grows. Forty years ago when I was a medical student, my hospital routinely prescribed lead and opium pills for gastro-intestinal upsets, and calomel, containing mercury, was given as a teething powder. I need hardly say that these medicines are no longer used. And with the decline in the prescription by doctors of mercury, the level of mercury in our rivers has gone down. At the same time, I am told, the level of steroids in our rivers has gone up because of the widespread use of the 'pill'! Are we now to be warned about the risk of getting cancer from the drinking of water, and to give up the 'pill' and risk pregnancies?

Without the wise development and application of more technology, there cannot be economic growth, and without economic growth it will be impossible to satisfy the aspirations of the vast majority of the world's population for a better life, any more than there will be the resources to deal with problems of the environment. As Michael Shanks put it in a recent broadcast,[3]

> If industry is now being set strict standards in its social and environmental behaviour, this is not because it has failed, but because it has largely succeeded in the tasks which society set it in the past. It is because industry has been so good, by and large, in meeting our basic needs for consumer goods, food, clothing, and so on, that we now demand something more.

And, one can add, it is because industry has produced the necessary resources that we expect our new demands to be met. Governments and environmentalists' movements do not create wealth – only industry does, whether primary or manufacturing. What we all want is more wealth – but we want it without running the risk of damaging the environment.

More resources constitute one of the critical keys for the safeguarding of the environment and of our amenities. Well into the nineteenth century most English cities lacked any adequate system for disposing of refuse and sewage. This was not because people did not appreciate the lack. Most were habituated to the filth of the streets, to open sewers, to polluted water; and they also knew that these things encouraged vermin and helped spread disease. Nothing was done because, given the social institutions of the period, and the way the wealth created by the industrial revolution was then distributed, both the resources and the political will to insist on the provision of a proper sewerage system were lacking. The village in which I live is only now being connected to a public sewerage system, and some neighbouring villages still have cess pits and septic tanks – to which I may say we had all been accustomed. No village Hampden got up to demand that we be connected to main sewers!

Long before the end of the nineteenth century both rich and poor suffered from the discomfort and danger to health of black fogs, caused mainly by the burning of soft coal in open grates. But it was not until 1956 that technological progress and the resources it made available made it both politically desirable and economically possible to prohibit this practice in English cities. Again it was not until the 1930s that the authorities were able to start correcting the visual pollution of public streets by wires and cables. The money to put telegraph wires and electricity cables underground was simply not there before. Of course, more is wanted than an economic surplus to correct these things. We shall always need the will to devote a proper part of our economic surplus to improving the environment, instead of spending all of it on more consumer goods and services and more leisure. This is what much of the current political concern over pollution is about. It is misguided to think of economic growth as something which is necessarily in conflict with the improvement of the environment.

Only better technology can eliminate the undesirable side-effects of bad technology, and it can do this only when the necessary resources become available. Social pressures encourage new technologies, and we should always try to assess these both scientifically and dispassionately – otherwise we are bound to get our priorities wrong. Technological miracles are always possible, but they are not inevitable. The basic question is always whether technological innovation occurs in response to need or whether, when successful, it merely creates new demand. There is an enormous literature on this subject, about which I do not propose saying more than a few words in this lecture.

In his Nuffield Lecture of 1969, G.A.H. Cadbury[4] argued convincingly that the mainspring of technological change is demand, and he illustrated this view in several ways. For example, television, as he pointed out, fitted much more adequately into the developing leisure pattern of the thirties, than did home films, the development of which in due course it killed. Another of Cadbury's examples was the technological changes in the textile industry which occurred in the earlier part of the industrial revolution and which were stimulated by the shortage of yarn and of labour. Cadbury also pointed to developments that have failed because they were ahead of their time, that is because they emerged before there was any sign of demand. For example, when Charles Babbage was working at the beginning of the nineteenth century, there was no demand for his 'difference and analytical engines', which are the forerunner of the modern computer. Cadbury also points out how the market mechanism and new demand lead to the substitution of new materials for old. But equally, he warns about the dangers of extrapolating present trends, and about trying to predict when, where, and how a particular and needed technological development will occur.

While all this is true, it is obvious that new and major technological developments will also inevitably occur before any particular need has been recognised, and equally that demand can be far too vague to indicate the nature of the technological development by which it is likely to be satisfied. On this point I have written elsewhere that it was clearly not the consumer who dreamed up the idea of television, or of supersonic transport aircraft, or of antibiotics. Moreover, where totally new products are concerned, the customer has to be persuaded that he wants them. For in spite of the stimulation of his appetite for the new product, through advertising and other forms of sales pressure, the customer may always fail to buy. It is because the consumer has the last word, and because modern technology has become so complex and costly, that every effort has to be made to plan not only the productive process, but also the market. The relentless progress of technology is as much determined by competition between producers to improve the nature and quality of their goods, that is to say, by competition in technical innovation, as it is by competition to gratify the wants and stimulate the appetite of the consumer with new things. But either way, it is clear that the process is not conditioned at its start by any broad conception of what the environment of man's future should be. From that point of view the process often seems blind. If supersonic flight is supposedly wanted, let there be supersonic flight – and leave the secondary problems which it will generate to be sorted out in due course. That is the way we operate. If plastic bags make the handling of fertiliser easier, use them instead of the old-fashioned sack, even if they become a kind of indestructible litter. The immediate satisfaction of the individual has almost always come first. If the benefits are undiluted, well and good. If secondary problems arise, they have to be dealt with later. This is the way many technological developments seem to have gone so far.

But it is essentially these secondary problems which build up into those matters of social concern on which Professor Beesley focused and which have to be dealt with by the diversion of effort, and usually of new resources as well. The social costs involved have hitherto been dealt with mainly by the tax payer, and not by the industry or public service whose actions have made it necessary that they be met. But the movement to internalise social costs is well under way, as both Mr. Peter Walker and Professor Beesley pointed out. Obviously there still remain a number of highly important questions to be answered before the job can be properly done. My own view is that the closer one can get to the source of 'pollution', whether it be in the testing of a new drug or in discovering the source of some toxic effluent, the easier the task of dealing with the problem. It is for this reason that I associated myself with Professor Beckerman in a Minority Report of British Estuaries and Coastal Waters to the Third Report of the Royal Commission on Environmental Pollution.[5] Like all those who write minority reports, I wondered at the time why the majority did not agree with us. My own reasons were simple enough, and they apply over a very wide field. First, I believe that pollution, like all disbenefits, should be reduced to the point where the costs of doing so are covered by the benefits arising from its reduction. I do not mind that one cannot easily define 'marginal social costs', or that there is difficulty in comparing different disbenefits. My argument begins once a particular disbenefit has been declared to be something that should be eliminated. Once this has been done, I do not believe that statutory controls or regulations can be rational if their effects cannot be measured precisely. All statutory controls on the discharge of toxic effluents necessitate the technological devices for recognising them, and measures for monitoring them. Once these are available, it is a matter of common-sense that the individuals who might have to bear the charge as 'polluters' would like their bill reduced, in the same way as all producers are concerned to lower the cost of any component of production. The advantage is always with the producer who in the end charges less for his products. But I do not want to go over all the arguments. They are set out adequately in the Report of the Royal Commission.

We have heard a great deal about cost-effective analyses, analyses which aim to show in advance which of alternative approaches to the production of a piece of equipment, or the achievement of some other given purpose, is the most economic. We have also learnt from bitter experience about the short-comings of such analyses. We have heard about cost-benefit analyses, a matter to which Professor Beesley directed much of his attention in his lecture. But when one tackles the theme I have been set, that is to say the role of technology in serving general social ends, the essential question is risk-benefit. Cost-benefit implies the evaluation of the benefits and costs of some piece of proposed action, and is thus admittedly a much wider concept than the traditional analysis which involves only economic factors. But risk-benefit deals with that category of cost-benefit or benefit-cost where the risk to life and health are the important components of cost. How many people are going to benefit or gain from doing something, or not doing something, in relation to the number who suffer? Is it wiser to spend X units of resources in order to prolong the lives of Y people suffering from some fearful disease, when the same degree of effort could possibly help 10Y people suffering from some other disease? A most important illustration of risk-benefit today is DDT. It is now under a cloud, essentially because the chemical accumulates in the tissues and because it has been shown to affect the reproductive processes of certain birds. To the best of my knowledge, however, no one in the course of the thirty years in which DDT has been used has shown that it has any deleterious effect on a human being. Yet because of the scare about DDT in the United States, a scare which has spread to other advanced countries, we find ourselves in the position of condemning a technological development which, in the words of

Dr. Borlaug, whose contributions to the improvement of agriculture in the underdeveloped and starving areas of the world was recognised by the award of the Nobel prize, is a unique contribution to the relief of human suffering.

I do not apologise for talking generalities. As I said at the start, I do not intend in this address to try my hand at a blueprint of how technology could bring peace on earth. What I have been concerned to show is that technology cannot of itself define social ends, any more than it can solve the major problems which face human society — problems such as the distribution of wealth, the elimination of starvation, and the end of war. Technology cannot even solve all definable social needs to which it may seem to be relevant. While it sometimes leaps ahead of scientific knowledge, it is in general based only on the common knowledge we all share. The resources for developing new technology are not inexhaustible, and priorities, as I must again insist, have to be agreed through the usual political processes. It is inexcusable when the slogan 'environment' is used by small minorities in order to foster what others can justifiably regard as selfish interests. These minorities are not the only ones who are concerned to see that the physical environment of tomorrow is one which is likely to be acceptable to the citizens of tomorrow. All rational people surely appreciate that the exponential growth of populations, all imbued with the desire for an exponential increase in their standard of living, is an impossible dream when viewed against a backdrop of a finite supply of resources. All thinking people are at least as much concerned as may be the numbers of the Club of Rome with the human good. Some of them, I suspect, are somewhat more sophisticated in appreciating the differences between human society, viewed as a system, and some complicated piece of machinery, which would be bound to break down if one of its critical cogs failed.   .

But, in my view, Professor Beesley was pointing the right lesson when he said that it was the business of government to define social needs. We always have to remember that in a democracy government usually acts and reacts mainly to public pressures. Politics is defined as 'the art of the possible'. From my own experience I myself prefer to regard it as the art of the transitional, and the art of dealing with the unexpected. When it comes to defining matters of social need, our government is well served — even if it may not have the resources to deal with all of them adequately. In addition to a highly trained civil service of policy makers, it employs a powerful scientific civil service which, certainly in the Departments of Enivronment, of Health and Social Security, and of Agriculture and Fisheries, to cite only three, is increasingly aware of the social problems of today and of those which lie ahead. I have been asked to say whether I believe that the changes which have resulted from last year's discussion of the organisation of government research and development will produce a more effective service. I sincerely hope they will, but at the same time we should expect the government's policy makers, whether or not they are scientists, to assess all the needs. They too have to respond to pressures, and to make judgements within the constraints of available knowledge and resources. It is of the utmost importance therefore that we also draw to the maximum extent possible on help from the universities and other learned institutions in determining our environmental demands.

Unfortunately, however, the science which is concerned in defining social needs can hardly be described as glamorous when compared with the sort of science which gets people elected to The Royal Society, or which on occasion merits the award of a Nobel prize. We do not have many departments of toxicology that are equipped to carry out the expensive routine work which is entailed in the definition of risks from chemicals used as drugs or food additives. There are not many departments of food science. Not all statisticians who attempt to define public health risks are as well-trained, and as critical as they might be, when it comes to differentiating between correlation and causation – in spite of the brilliant demonstration of how this should be done in the instance of the relation of cigarette-smoking to cancer. All one can hope, therefore, is that social needs will be discussed more and more in the dispassionate and rational atmosphere of the scientific forum, and that university departments will become more and more ready to take up the challenge and to help find the technical solutions to these needs.

I have already said that I agree broadly with the proposition that it is demand which stimulates technological innovation. On the other hand, one has to be careful lest demand encourages 'instant technology'. Recently I had to comment on the new American programme to 'conquer cancer', and made the general observation that while the injection of vast new funds would certainly increase the pace of biomedical research, it could never guarantee the discovery of a cure.[6] Money does not buy the galvanising ideas which transform basic knowledge. The newspapers have recently reported an equally ambitious American proposal to carry out the research necessary to harness solar power, a programme which calls for the expenditure of an average of \$350 million a year over the next ten years. There is obviously a social need to achieve the aim of this programme, and without this new initiative, progress would obviously be slower than otherwise. But equally, it is hazardous to predict, as I have already said, if, when, and how success will come. It is salutory to note that it is already all but agreed that the technological developments into which the motor industry of the United States has been impelled in order to meet the statutory standards for emission in 1976 will lead to cars being fitted with catalytic devices which are highly expensive but which are also unlikely to work. New technology operates on the fringes of knowledge. The costly failures which have characterised new technology in the defence field over the past twenty years should warn us about what might happen in the civil field if we rush forwards blindly.

Let me conclude with a few more generalitities. We have reached our present level of civilisation largely because of science and technology. Through science and education we have also been raised to a higher level of awareness about the dangers which mankind now faces. But each generation operates on a different level of awareness. The eighteenth-century inhabitants of London tolerated a social and technological environment which we would not endure. I would hazard a guess that the average Londoner of that time would have avidly exchanged his dwelling for a house in the neighbourhood of London Airport — regardless of the noise about which we complain today. We cannot say what the risks of tomorrow will be, or what our successors will regard as a good environment and a good way of life. All we can hope is that the decisions that we take today will not be prejudicial to those who follow us. We have to differentiate between the concepts of risk-benefit, cost-benefit, and cost-effectiveness. Society at large takes decisions about the latter two. Because of his more exact and specialised knowledge, it is the scientist's job to provide a rational assessment of risk-benefit. We also need to remember that resources are always scarce, and that the decisions which are taken now about social values must not be such as to constrain economic growth. It would surely be better to spur growth by encouraging wise technological developments, than to risk the plague, famine, revolution and internecine war which would inevitably break out were we to try – and I do not know who the 'we' are – to impose direct constraints on human breeding and on a share-out of the wealth that already exists.

Obviously if population does not stop growing at an exponential rate, man's social and political problems will become more and more difficult. But there *are* social feed-backs in human society. The most recent indications are that in the few years since population growth became a matter of public concern in the United States, the birth-rate of that country has all but reached zero replacement level. Equally, if non-renewable resources are used without care for the future, we shall also be in trouble – even though we know that technological developments have, over the years, always reacted to need by producing replaceable materials. And experience shows that pollution and devastation can be cleared up, given the will and resources, and given that we can reconcile conflicting views about what constitutes pollution and what constitutes amenity.

But we must not think we are gods. Our generation did not start pollution. Nor, as the geological history of our planet shows only too well, were we the first to change the landscape. The world of the Tertiary looked totally different from that of today. The ice-caps once devastated the land surface of Britain. Long before man ever evolved, a thousand times more species than exist now were eliminated from the systematist's catalogue. We also know that the life of the sun, the life of the star around which our planet moves, is in astronomical terms, finite, and that some time, billions of years ahead, and like thousands of other planets before it, our own will die. We know that whatever is done to eliminate the hazards of life, we shall remain mortal. And we also know that there are laws of thermo-dynamics against which no parliament can legislate. Somehow or other we have to live within these constraints. If we no longer throw pollutants into the sky, or into the rivers and sea, or on to the land, we still have to find a way of dealing with them. They will not disappear of their own accord.

In a lecture which Bertrand Russell delivered nearly twenty-five years ago,[7] he remarked that we were then in a phase of lethargic and irrational despair, beset by some kind of death wish. 'Everyone knows', to quote his own words,

> how some primitive communities, brought suddenly into contact with white men, become listless, and finally die from mere absence of the will to live. In Western Europe, the new conditions of danger which exist are having something of the same effect. Facing facts is painful, and the way out is not clear. Nostalgia takes the place of energy directed towards the future. There is a tendency to shrug the

shoulders and say, 'Oh well, if we are exterminated by hydrogen bombs, it will save a lot of trouble'.

He then went on to say that:

Mankind is in the position of a man climbing a difficult and dangerous precipice, at the summit of which there is a plateau of delicious mountain meadows. With every step that he climbs, his fall, if he does fall, becomes more terrible; with every step his weariness increases and the ascent grows more difficult. Does the exhausted climber make one more effort, or does he let himself sink into the abyss? ..... We are in the middle of a race between human skill as to means and human folly as to ends.

Today the exhaustion of resources, the issues of pollution and the environment, and of population growth, seem to have taken the place of hydrogen bombs as the prevailing social fear. But we need not, indeed we dare not, despair. We *shall* deal with these problems — because we simply have to. That, at any rate, is my philosophy. And that, in my view, is the continuing role of technology.

NOTES

1 *The Limits to Growth,* D.H. Meadows, D.L. Meadows, J. Randers, and W.W. Behrens III, Universe Books, New York, 1972.

2 S. Zuckerman, 'Science, Technology, and Environmental Management', in *Who Speaks for Earth?,* M.F. Strong (ed.), W.W. Norton & Company Inc., New York, 1973, pp.129-50.

3 M. Shanks, 'Capitalism in Doubt', *The Listener,* 8

March 1973, pp.300-302.

4 G.A.H. Cadbury, *Our Technological Future* (The 1969 Viscount Nuffield Memorial Paper), Preprint, The Institution of Production Engineers, 1969.

5 Cmnd. 5054, HMSO, London, September 1972.

6 *Cancer Research*, A Report by Lord Zuckerman, HMSO, London, 1972.

7 Republished in his book *The Impact of Science on Society*, George Allen & Unwin, London, 1952.

FIVE

Education for Corporate Responsibility

P.F. NIND

Forty-five years ago Alfred Zimmern wrote:
> Civilisation is control over environment. A civilised man is a man who understands the world in which he is living and the forces by which it is moved... A civilised society is a society equipped with the knowledge to control its environment...[1]

In 1962 the Federation of British Industries appointed a working party to investigate the management education and training needs of industry. The report[2] made clear that industry's immediate needs were to remedy the shortcomings of the education system at each of its stages — primary, secondary and tertiary — brought about by the omission of some essentials, adequate mathematics for instance, or by the commission of mistakes such as too early specialisation. In other words, management education could not be isolated from other stages and fields of education.

In the same way, in this fourth Stockton Lecture I have decided to interpret 'education for corporate responsibility' broadly rather than in depth, because the phrase has little meaning outside the context of, first, the whole education process itself and, second, the relationship between the individual citizen and society.

89

Social responsibility is both a personal and a corporate matter. Each of us plays a dual role. Our attitude to society stems from within ourselves as individuals and is personal to us. But nearly all our activities are played on a corporate stage, through corporate groups. To speak of corporate responsibility therefore is to mean the responsibility of groups of individuals towards a society which those same individuals also judge from their own personal viewpoint. Group or individual — they are as one but in separate roles.

Formal education for corporate responsibility therefore covers no more than one corner of the education canvas. If in essentials it appears to conflict with the educational preparation which individuals need in order to play their individual role in society, there must be something seriously wrong with the structure of the education system or with the philosophy which pervades it. It is, accordingly, questions about this system and philosophy which we must first ask.

The phrase, education for corporate responsibility, presupposes that we have agreed on the kind of society within which we seek to be responsible. It suggests that there may be a difference of standards between the private individual's responsibility and that of the group or corporation. It may even imply that education is a process which distills responsibility with ingredients which vary according to the individual or corporate mould in which they are mixed. But whatever presuppositions there have to be, we must start from the fact that at one end we have society itself, at the other the private individuals which make up that society. From opposite ends of the spectrum, the individual and society are linked by two things: by the permutations and combinations of groups, constantly changing, which give the technological age its corporate character; and by the educational system, which seeks to prepare the individual for his place both in society itself and within the groups which comprise it. The way the individuals are educated will influence the qualitative content, and the direction and speed of change, of that society; equally, society's corporate character will inevitably influence the content and the structure of the educational system through which the individuals have to pass.

It is apparent that in considering the kind of society we want, we are faced by three dissonant factors. First, the fundamental democratic belief that all men are born equal implies the right of each man not only to feel that he can judge the issues of the day as well as his neighbour but also to translate his feelings into action, political and industrial; whereas of course all men are not born of equal ability, and somehow we have to find the best way of helping the ablest to come through the mass without preventing the rest from in turn reaching their own level of potentiality. Secondly, modern life is so massively intricate and technically complicated that only a limited number of people can fully understand the intricacies and complications and the possible solutions to them, and society can only afford a limited number of chiefs for the mass of indians – which in turn inevitably offends the egalitarian philosophy of today. Thirdly, and more controversially, the developed countries (the market leaders of the modern age) now encapsulate and foster an acquisitive attitude towards life which the advertising media exploit, which takes all too little account of environmental and other social responsibilities, and which rates the exoticism of material gain much higher than the

Aristotelian values.

Education cannot be divorced from the wider issues of morality, which is why it must be deeply concerned with the quality of life. The ethical standards a society abides by both set the pattern of the educational system, in its goals, and its media for reaching them, and in turn is influenced and adjusted by the experience and moral balance of those coming through it into the world, where they will themselves be setting the standards for the next generation. For us in Britain there are three problems here. First, moral standards in the field of corporate activity tend to be regarded as the responsibility of someone else – the boss, the government, the law, but rarely of the man or the manager on the spot who has to take the decision, and this leads to a deep dichotomy between the spirit and its interpretation. There is evidence at some of the business schools that top management is now profoundly concerned with these attitudes and how to overcome them, and that graduate students are equally aware of the dangers; but that there is much less consciousness of the part of middle management, which means the engine room of our corporate society. Secondly, in terms of the market-place where most of us act out our lives, talk of moral codes of action tends to imply a recourse to religious activity which can, paradoxically, inhibit the finding of constructive solutions. Thirdly, we have the reality behind Dean Acheson's comment that Britain had lost an empire but had not yet found a new role. Our education system was part of a machine which needed helmsmen to take it to the five continents of the world, *gubernatores* to control distant countries and rule their peoples by a kind of benevolent divine right. It has taken many years for this characteristic spirit of empire to be eradicated from the minds of the teachers and the taught, and the vacuum left by the aftermath has only recently started to be filled by a new educational consciousness.

Amongst its other targets and charges, education must provide some form of social responsibility. In a speech on 25th January the Prime Minister suggested that, in its link with society, education 'has at once a conservative and a radical function: to preserve and transmit the human skills, sympathies, and values which no external changes can render obsolete: and at the same time to foster the capacity for research and invention, to encourage re- sourcefulness, adaptability, and a broad perspective, and to nourish the habit of decisive action.'[3] I wonder whether his interpretation of these two functions goes deep enough. Are not the real questions: should educa- tion's aim be to provide social stability or social change? Can it do both equally well at the same time, or are there alternating phases? For in a sense they are antithetical, and perhaps it is the inability to find what many would consider to be the impossible compromise which lies at the heart of so much of educational controversy in our time. However, in the context of the social balance between productivity and amenity which we are seeking, it is important that we should ask these questions and understand why there are no simple answers to them.

And there are other questions we should be asking. As well as seeking how education can contribute towards the achievement of this social balance, ought we not also to be analysing now constructive social policies such as environmental conservation and the prevention of pollu- tion should be influencing the future pattern and philosophy of our education? And if education has a major part to play in improving the quality of life in the future is it not worthwhile to enquire whether and how educational shortcomings in the past may have contributed to the disastrous decay of life's quality we see around us today?

At the Meeting of the British Association for the Advancement of Science at Cambridge in September 1965, John Dancy delivered a presidential address[4] to the Education section on the philosophy of technical education, in which he argues that the idea that technology and liberal education are incompatible is wrong, 'that on the contrary some experience of technology is an essential ingredient within a liberal education.' He says that 'it is a misconception that the Ancient Greeks scorned technology.' Almost the reverse is true. The members of the world's first great scientific school, in Ionia in the sixth and fifth centuries BC, 'had both their physics and their metaphysics firmly grounded in techniques.' And Sophocles placed his list of the great human achievements in this order: 'shipbuilding, agriculture, speech, urban life, housebuilding... a jumble in which the progress of civilisation and culture is shown to be inextricably bound up with advances in technology.' According to Dancy it is not until the Renaissance that one finds again such a unity between art, science and technology – a unity which reached its apogee in Leonardo and 'which is the hallmark of all great civilisations of history'. But in the two thousand years between these two great periods another voice was heard, singing, says Dancy, 'a siren song that has beguiled Europe' ever since the Renaissance – the voice of Plato. Plato's whole approach to philosophy exalted the mind at the expense of the body, ideas over matter and theory over experiment.' It helped to produced 'a snobbish attitude to applied science which runs like an ugly thread through the history of European thought' and which itself helped to polarise the evils of the industrial revolution which have been left to us as such a burdensome legacy today. It had a particularly strong influence upon the English theory and practice of education during the nineteenth century and has left it still suffering from 'two correlated hierarchies, one of learning, one of men'. To Plato the activities of the mind are stratified. 'At the top is *pure* mathematics, which gives *pure* knowledge of the *pure* world of ideas. At the bottom are the *mere* practical arts which give *mere* opinion about the *mere* world of the senses' — the category in which he placed technology. Secondly, society was stratified to match the gradations of learning. 'Plato's caste society runs from the philospher-kings at the top to there mere artisans at the bottom. For Plato was social and intellectual snob rolled into one, a combination,' says Dancy, 'irresistible to the English. *His* intellectual theory matched and reinforced *our* traditional social practice.'

Plato's malevolent influence on British education, and on social attitudes within the darker context of the industrial revolution, was emphatic. The reaction against its consequences has been amongst the factors leading to the cravings for egalitarianism which, as we have seen in recent years, has sown the seeds of dissension and confusion. The time has come perhaps to tilt opinion a little in the other direction, and in this context I want to touch upon two important subjective notions whose values have for some time been impaired by popular undercurrents of emotionalism — leadership, and the concept of élitism.

The balance between productivity and amenity must inevitably be a fine one, and its successful achievement will depend upon the quality of leadership provided within all the estates of the realm (to use Michael Beesley's phrase) — central and local government, and industry.

On 1 February the Danish minority Government, under its new Prime Minister, Anker Joergensen, survived by two votes an Opposition motion censuring it for the result of its negotiations on agricultural compensation within the EEC. The critics said that the Prime Minister was too occupied with his longer term plans to have time to attend to the daily business of government, and one of the party leaders wrote in a newspaper article: 'Some experienced politicians in the Government should gently take Anker by the hand and quietly tell him what politics are all about before too much damage is done.'[5] In terms of our theme in these lectures, and as an interpretation of 'what politics are all about', this is a horrifying comment. But it does illustrate that if the quality of our life up to the end of this century and beyond is not to deteriorate, society must be able to generate leaders of high quality. This will largely depend upon our education system being able, much more effectively than hitherto, to develop the potential of each individual at those moments in his life when that potential is ripe for development and through programmes more appropriate for the two ends of the spectrum we noted at the beginning — the individual himself, and society as the corporate whole.

Ironically, the democratic process itself militates against a fully effective maximisation of environmental planning. A long term strategy which will ultimately benefit everyone may inevitably have short-term disadvantages for some, and politicians are hostages to electoral fortune every three or four years. How far is a self-imposed discipline possible, and is there a sufficient will both to supply and to accept the kind of leadership which today's participative and increasingly egalitarian society needs? I suspect that in the political arena, where all the big issues must rightly be fought out, we have currently too much of the Plaza Toro style of leadership – the Duke, you remember,

Led his regiment from behind –

He found it less exciting.

It is apposite in this context to consider the styles of leadership of the present leader of the Labour Party and his predecessor. Of Hugh Gaitskell, Roy Jenkins has written: 'He believed that a leader should point the way and not merely follow bursts of transient opinion, whether they came from inside or outside the Labour Party.'[6] And in an article[7] last January the Political Editor of the *Financial Times* wrote that Gaitskell, 'having started off with certain fundamental ideals of social justice, then proceeded with rigorous care to think out the consequences of an egalitarian position in a way which Harold Wilson has never been able, or perhaps wished, to do.' Curiously enough this in fact made him more radical and more democratic than his successor. His methods, too, were 'the reverse of the élitism with which he has sometimes been charged, for it was the product of a calm belief that people are quite capable of understanding sophisticated arguments and responding to them,' and by being of course prepared to listen to the force of logic rather than of expediency.

Leadership needs to be learnéd leadership rather than informed leadership. Everyone today believes himself to be informed, pounded as he is by the mass media. But leadership, and the decision-making which is its instrument and its ultimate justification, must be based on study and education and the knowledge of techniques. As Stephen Roskill has written: 'What is certain is that today the educational requirements of the leader are heavier than ever before.' He must not only keep abreast of technical developments, but his social and human responsibilities oblige him 'to reap the harvest of wisdom and understanding broadly known as the "humanities".'[8] Hence the importance of steady and continuous self-education.

The extreme proponents of educational egalitarianism fear any other system than a free-for-all because it may produce a kind of self-perpetuating élite. But the mistake they make is to try to wield the educational system as a weapon to overcome economic inequalities and social injustices, thereby in turn destroying some of the key qualities of achievement and learning which are so desperately needed as the criteria against which we should be setting our standards of attainment in a world flooded with so many shoddy standards. Equality of opportunity there must be, but the educational system can best strive for this by winnowing at every stage so that each human grain can fall onto a patch of ground where it will find the soil most favourable to its growth at that particular season. Some plants, let us remember, need bedding out later than others.

I doubt whether society's need for larger numbers of talented, educated men and women can be satisfied by our present post-secondary system of education, which is wasteful, expensive and inequitable. In a recent radio broadcast[9] Lord Balogh argued that our élite, personified for him by the corps of top civil servants, is too conformist, that our leadership therefore suffers from an absence of entrepreneurial talents, of innovators. If this is true it is perhaps because, firstly, the system pays too much attention to the dictates of breeding first-class honours graduates at the age of twenty-one – early academic developers do not necessarily turn into the kind of people who have the requisite entrepreneurial flair or the will to take innovative initiatives during their forties and fifties when they will be expected to reach positions of influence and responsibility. And secondly, the education system does not sufficiently well cater for the later developer who showed neither the inclination nor the ability to tread the still too narrow academic paths during the immediately post-secondary phase.

During the past year there has been a plethora of reports on education, of papers white and green. It is a sad reflection on current values that so much of the critical flame of these reports, in the press and elsewhere, has been spent on statistics, percentages and ratios, on the bricks and mortar, and so little on the concepts, ideas and philosophy. This lecture is not the place to discuss whether the binary system is good or bad, or the merits of the comprehensive polyversity, but some aspects of the post-secondary educational controversy are germane to our theme.

In his January speech the Prime Minister said that 'it is becoming increasingly absurd to think of education as a process which stops at fifteen or eighteen or twenty-two. Indeed, the more we improve the methods and the institutions for educating the young, the greater the need, and the demand, for continuing education later.'[10] In his Dimbleby Lecture last autumn Noel Annan stressed that it is 'mistaken kindness to make higher education available to anyone who says he wants it, regardless of his ability to benefit from it... It is cruel because a student who hasn't learnt to read books and express himself ends, not through his own fault, humiliated by failure. It is also calamitous, because if you ask the university, or any institution, to perform tasks it can't do, you will distort and break it.'[11] In his Vice-Chancellor's oration at Oxford last October Sir Alan Bullock affirmed that 'the demand for increased opportunities for continuing education after school will not only grow, but ought to be met to the limits that we can afford; it seems to me equally clear that this demand cannot be met by an indefinite expansion of university education, which would not only destroy the universities as we know them, but would fail to satisfy the diversity of needs and desires which lead people to seek education. What we need to create, surely, is a corresponding diversity of institutions, types of courses, qualifications required, and methods of learning and teaching.'[12]

These short extracts from three recent speeches signpost the directions in which new developments in post-secondary education might proceed. In particular there are two which are especially important in the context of our Stockton theme – a modular system of courses, and what Sir Kenneth Berrill called in his Birkbeck Foundation Oration[13] 'lifetime education' but which I prefer as 'continuing education' or the French *education permanente.*

The Government White Paper of last December uses six expressions in connection with post-secondary education – further, advanced, higher, adult, tertiary and recurrent.[14] It goes on to describe, in an excellent section of the report, what these expressions are commonly understood to mean, but it then explains that 'the divisions indicated by these definitions are artificial in that they present different faces of a broadly organised effort to enable all members of society, with their widely differing aspirations and capacities, once they have left school behind them, to learn where, when and what they want in the way that best suits them.' It is clear that, despite appearances, British post-secondary education is extraordinarily inflexible. As one observer has put it, one of its restrictive features is 'the rigid categorisation of students by course and by mode of study and the preoccupation of institutions with a particular type of student or course.'[15] There is no ease of transfer between courses and ranges so that students may alter the direction, pace or mode of their study as circumstances change.

I believe that the only way to maximise a post-secondary system of education, for both the individual and society, is to break down the divisions to which the White Paper refers and to regard all education after leaving school as part of one system of continuing education to which all citizens of every age have access as and when their abilities and inclinations inspire them. The principal instrument to provide the necessary flexibility in a unitary system of continuing education is the module, combined with some form of credit transference. The advantages would be many, some of them lucidly explained by Berrill in his Birkbeck Lecture.[16]

1. Education should aim to keep alive an interest of enquiry and a desire to learn. It is arguable that compulsory education up to sixteen kills this spirit of inquiry in too many young people and

that the age limit should be reduced rather than extended. A unitary system of continuing education could help to change the attitude towards the early school-leaver which at present makes him feel inferior.

2. It would ease the pressure on sixth forms and their in some cases still too narrow, specialist curricula, and it might help to discourage schools from cramming for university places some of their students who are quite unsuitable for post-school university-type courses but who would benefit from a later less violent introduction to higher education – to quote Noel Annan:[17]

> there are many boys and girls who cannot reach university standard at the age of eighteen but who later in life develop their full capacity and can fully benefit from high-level professional courses at a university, or indeed elsewhere.

3. The number of university graduates is increasing faster than the number of graduate-identified jobs, thus leaving a trail of dissatisfied graduates. Students would gain more from their higher education if, maturer and more motivated, they hopped on the educational wagon at moments and the speed of their own choice – in contrast, as Berrill puts it, with some young people who 'ride along on the escalator of continued education with very little vision of the relevance of what they are doing to their future working life.'[18]

4. From the purely educational point of view it would be more efficient. It is not possible to pull

all one person's requirement of knowledge and skills into one cycle of education – new interests, new specialisms will develop; retraining is needed to take care of the changes in industrial structures and technologies.

5. The academically-minded early developer will continue to follow immediate post-school courses at universities. But the majority of people will want a practice-oriented type of education – languages, physical sciences, engineering, management and social sciences, etc. for which a modular system of continuing education would be wholly appropriate. Many students find after a while at university that they are studying the wrong subjects, and they would be able to transfer more easily to others – something particularly important to the growing field of environmental studies and sciences with their varied ingredients of technology, planning, experience and social acceptability.

6. It would help to break down the rigid binary borders of higher education and open up greater flexibility of movement both of students through the credit system, and of faculty.

7. It would perhaps enable programmes to meet changing demands more sensitively and quickly and provide greater flexibility for curriculum development and reform, which the Open University has shown can lead down many valuable and interesting avenues. Once again this is important for environmental studies which should now be entering the curricula of many physical and social

science programmes.*

8.   It would be a more equitable system, bearing in mind the large numbers of adults today whom higher education has passed by, without much hope of their catching up.

9.   Lastly, I am convinced it would be less wasteful of money. In commending the expansion of lifetime vocational education Berrill hoists the storm-cone of cost. But I believe that the increase in costs need only be marginal because there would be fewer immediate post-school students at the universities and polytechnics, there would be fewer drop-outs and the modular system might well enable the physical resources and facilities to be used more economically across the full twelve months of the year. I wonder, too, whether such a system would not allow more easily a proportion of the financing through students' loans.

The kind of continuing education system to aim for is summed up by the recent report of the Commission of Post-Secondary Education in Ontario, 'The Learning Society,' which proposes 'an accessible hierarchy of educational services, with screens but not closed barriers between the different levels' and which identifies the six

---

*One such type of reform, but at the sixth-form level, has been pioneered by the new Nuffield Physical Science programme which has built into it an important feature providing for students of different levels of ability, so that a weaker student can concentrate on essentials without distraction or examination penalty — an approach to programmes which is governed not by the marking of class results but by the provision of different levels of curricula according to aptitude and ability.

basic principles of universal access, diversity, flexibility, transferability, equity and public accountability.

The field where the modular system of continuing education has developed furthest is that of management education, with its many programmes of varying length from bachelor's degree courses in the management sciences, master's degree programmes, HND and DMS courses, part-time and full-time, to post-experience courses of from one year (the Sloan programme) to a few days. Just as there is constant interaction between society and the individual on the one hand and the education system itself on the other, so in the management education field there should be a reciprocal state of creative tension between the system and its clients, both individual and corporate. If industry's overt needs and demands are for techniques in profit maximisation, financial control, market research, etc. — those are what the system will provide, adding perhaps its own conceptual contributions in the spheres of business policy and of the structure of organisations. But judging by recent developments such as the interim report of the CBI's Company Affairs Committee under Lord Watkinson I suspect that a social policy groundswell will soon be lapping around the gunwales of company boardrooms, and the management education system must be prepared to accept the challenge. Indeed some of the business schools, such as Durham and Manchester with their Joint Development Activities, are already making a seminal contribution towards solving some of the abrasive social conflicts of our time.

If, as one observer has put it, 'more radical changes are likely to be needed than schemes for profit-sharing, capital-sharing, employee shareholding and wider share

ownership',[19] the education system must be drawn into
the arena and I have no doubt that through the
combination of their research, consultancy and teaching
roles the business schools will be able to provide a
powerful reinforcement to Government and to industrial
corporations. It is not so many years ago that to find a
personnel director on a company board was the excep-
tion rather than the rule and we look back in bewilder-
ment if not anger that this was so. In the years to come I
have no doubt that we shall see the social policies
director in the boardroom — perhaps in the quantifiable
job of social responsibility auditor as John Humble has
suggested, but whatever form his job takes 'there must
be, and be seen to be,' in the words of the Watkinson
committee, 'an ethical dimension in corporate activity.
Companies must in our view recognise that they have
functions, duties and moral obligations that go beyond
the immediate pursuit of profit and the requirements of
the law.' I should like to see this director appointed
in some cases from amongst the top academic staff of
business schools. This will be a new field for development and the feed-back into the teaching at the schools
would be of paramount importance.

One of the estates of the realm we have not yet
mentioned is that of the trade unions. Except perhaps for
the Israeli Histadruth, the British trade union movement
is the most powerful in the free world. No social or
corporate policies can be nationally effective without a
constructive contribution from the unions. Because of
their historical background and because of the present
dangerous polarisation of politics in terms of an updated
class struggle (with the multi-nationals, property specula-
tors and the bureaucracy paradigmatically replacing the

landed aristocracy and the individual mill-owners of the nineteenth century) the unions will find it very difficult to make the contribution which I am sure they would wish to make. Nowhere is the importance of leadership, which we discussed earlier, more important than here.

I am one of those who believe that the harshest acerbities of our industrial relations on a national level will never disappear until, to speak in metaphor, the two-sided bargaining table is abolished and replaced by a round one. But even without such basic structural changes much can be done, which is not being done, to improve industrial relations. Where on a national or regional scale are the vital industrial and social problems of the day being discussed conceptually, constructively, in a neutral environment, by the representatives of government, management and the unions? If union leaders will not go to business schools in any numbers, understandably perhaps, for fear of being thought to be bought by the bosses in the minds of their members, one or more new institutions must be established where such activities can take place in unequivocally open and responsible surroundings. The percipient amongst union leaders are fully aware of the value of business school-type programmes, not only for learning techniques and understanding in greater depth the scale and complexities of industrial and national problems but also for the opportunity to enable the feelings and philosophies of the unions to be understood in an atmosphere conducive to constructive discussion. Whether or not the unions have their own training colleges is beside the point; it is the catalytic effect of all the elements in national and industrial life getting together for significantly long periods that is important — and perhaps most important of all at the middle and local levels where, as we have seen, on the management side there is less awareness of the social issues than at the top and amongst the youngest. Is it not remarkable that national strike succeeds national strike, year after year, yet there is no co-ordinated scientific attempt to study each strike, its cause, more importantly the day by day and hour by hour progress which led up to the final breach? If, a year or two after the end of a strike, when the temperature had cooled, some of the principal parties, government, union and management, could be brought together under academic chairmanship and research, to study the details, what went wrong and when and why, we could build up a formidable library of industrial relations lore through which many lessons for the future could be learnt.

What more can government, central and local, do in this field? The University Grants Committee have been generous in their provision of funds for the expansion of management education in the last and in the new quinquennia, but some local authorities have been myopic towards the formation and growth of the new Regional Management Centres where so much education and training can be done for local industries and for the staff of local government offices themselves. The attitude of the Civil Service towards some aspects of management development is equivocal.

In the second Stockton Lecture Michael Beesley stressed the importance of interchange of staff between the various estates — central and local government, and industry — and he suggested that this was partially an educational problem. Whether or not one believes that management is a profession, there are common features and techniques for the practice of managing people, no matter what the product or service provided. The business schools were established primarily for the needs of business, but their roles are already changing, as can be seen most clearly in the United States where, calling themselves management schools or schools of administration, many are devoting increasing activities to urban development and other public and non-profit-making fields.

When here in Britain it was decided, following the Fulton Report, that post-experience courses on a larger scale were appropriate for the career development of civil servants, a Civil Service Staff College was founded. In some fields, notably for the recently joined recruit, the College has done an excellent job. But, granted that this is still a new institution, feeling its way through the usual rough waters which every new craft has to experience, there are signs that it has not yet fulfilled the hopes which are due to the arguably ablest and certainly most important single body of men and women in the country. Whitehall's Sunningdale symphony sounds similar to the music which used to be played some years ago in the concert halls of the big corporations where the strings of the personnel departments had to battle it out with the brass and woodwind of the line departments. There were two problems: financial responsibility, and the value to be placed on releasing key staff for relatively long periods. As the value of training courses become more apparent, however, line departments were more willing, even anxious, to release their personnel, and training became an integral charge within specific cost centres. Perhaps the Civil Service Department and the departments of state will reach a similar working understanding. No

standards of teaching staff and resources can be too high
for the Civil Service.

But this is only half the matter; on management
courses at all management schools there should be an
appropriate mix of representatives from departments of
state, from local government, from education and health
services, as well as from business. How many environmental and urban problems, for instance, would be more
effectively handled if more of the personnel concerned
with them in each of the estates could have the
opportunity to pursue joint programmes in the objective,
analytical atmosphere of a management school? With
politicians continually having to reduce long-term plans
to meet the exigencies of periodic electoral campaigns the
skills, knowledge and decision-making propensities of the
administrators are of paramount importance and this
kind of formal training can only enhance them. However
talented our civil servants may be they need, at all levels
of seniority, the continual updating and "recyclage'
which is needed in any field of activity. Succeeding
Governments have placed increasing responsibilities on
the shoulders of the departments of state. It is up to
Government, therefore, to ensure that the administrators
are given the time and the incentive to take an active part
in the continuing education process, and that they are
provided with the best facilities to do this – within their
own institutions and at the management schools outside.

Turning to organisation within Whitehall, management
education is primarily the responsibility of the Department of Education and Science in conjunction mainly
with the UGC, the Social Science Research Council, and
the local authorities. The education and training of
managers is assuredly a close interest of the Department

of Trade and Industry and of the Department of Employment, but if the DTI has any influence on policies there is little evidence to the outside observer; this is regrettable. However, the body on which I shall like to focus particular attention is the SSRC.

In a striking article in *The Times* last January, on the relation of political thought to progress, Reginald Maudling wrote: 'We must recognise that... fundamental problems are being raised by the advance of science, and by the fact that our progress in the physical sciences is greatly outstripping our progress in the political sciences.'[20] And he continued: 'I believe the discoveries of biology and psychology are far more significant than nuclear physics or space travel, and they will inevitably raise fundamental questions of where authority should rest in society, and of the definition of moral attitude.' I would go further and say that there are problems of a social nature today which are infinitely more urgent and difficult to know how to tackle, let alone to solve, than any purely technological problem. The scientific hurdles for birth control have been surmounted; the social obstacles are far more formidable. From population control, through the soaring increase in crime, to our dogged inability to work together without constant friction within the corporate bodies in which most citizens of a developed nation have to operate, there is an increasing number of discordant social problems.

The research body under whose auspices this field of vital social subjects rests, including management education, is the SSRC. It has an enormous range to cover. For instance, input characteristics of ball-skill acquisition; concepts of disease and medical practices of Peruvian peasants; social determinants of belief studied in an

English community of nuns; financial data bank at the London Business School. These indicate the wide scope of the hundreds of projects for which the Council has to find funds. The Science Research Council has a budget this year, 1972/73, of £62,351,000. The Medical Research Council's budget is £24,853,000. The SSRC has to get by on £4,900,000! And a high proportion of even this small sum has to be set aside for postgraduate student grants. Is this really the value we place on trying to find out more about our social problems and how to solve them? In an article in the July 1972 number of *Minerva*, Andrew Shonfield, a former Chairman of the SSRC, implied that he might be satisfied with a modest £10,000,000.[21] My own view is that the SSRC covers too wide a field, and that as a first step its present Management and Industrial Relations Committee should be hived off into a separate Council with its own independent budget.

I want to finish by returning to some of the broader aspects of education. The educational nuts and bolts of the scales balancing productivity and amenity will be forged at the management schools where the merits of shareholders and employees and consumers, of techno-logical progress and economic growth and the environ-ment, will be discussed and researched and taught. But the effectiveness of all this will depend largely upon society, collectively and individually, being aware of the importance of the issues and how the already precarious balance can so easily and irrevocably be destroyed. We are far from achieving this sense of awareness.

The cornerstone is the human environment with all its associated problems; for if we cannot maintain an adequate physical quality of life, asset-stripping and other technical and ethical issues will be as mere blemishes on a pock-marked world. Spear-headed by the Government but with the close-columned aid of local authorities, of industry and of voluntary organisations, a co-ordinated educational programme covering every stage of education must be introduced and kept permanently up to pitch. An environmental perspective should be integrated into the education of all students at every level. In the words of the report[22] by one of the working parties set up by Peter Walker in preparation for the United Nations Conference on the Human Environment in Stockholm last year, education and information is needed to:

— understand the interrelationship of man and his environment;
— develop and impart the practical skills of managing the environment without destroying it at the same time;
— develop a non-exploitive ethic towards nature for its intrinsic values as well as its necessity for survival;
— make people aware of their rights and responsibilities towards common resources and develop social behaviour accordingly.

The need is to change values and attitudes as well as impart knowledge.

Up to the school-leaving age of sixteen an average of only 2½ hours per day is spent by a day-school child in a classroom. Yet for every hundred pounds spent inside the classroom only one is spent outside it. There is immense scope here for imaginative programmes with local authorities and local industry. Within the classroom, the Schools Council should encourage new curricula, both examinable and non-examinable. An example of the former is the excellent Environmental Studies 'A' level syllabus which the Wiltshire County Council is sponsoring through the Associated Examining Board. The aim of this syllabus is 'to provide a quantitative and objective approach to the environment and an appreciation of man's place within it, and his responsibility in the management of it.' There is a section on Energy, fundamental to the whole syllabus, so that the subject can be studied basically in terms of energy resources and energy flows. In the section on the management of the environment, the morphology of a specific city is studied. One of the main bottlenecks for all school programmes will be the shortage of suitably trained teachers and a massive attack to overcome this must be launched.

The part that local authorities, professional associations and industry can play has already been signposted by pilot projects. The Hammersmith Study, begun in 1969, involved the Polytechnic of Central London, the Architectural Association and the local borough planning office. On the industrial side IBM, RTZ and others have been associated with the Hampshire Education Authority in the Trident Project; and at Churchill College, Cambridge, the fourth Industrial Fellow Commoner from Shell, John Bury, is working on a study of Shell's Anglesey Marine Terminal project which will be providing a facility for the benefit of a large section of the community but at the potential risk of the local environment – the perfect example of our Stockton theme of seeking a social balance between productivity and amenity.

Starry-eyed idealism is of course the privilege of lovers, but I should hate to think that underlying the therapeutic exertions of our management schools there is not a determination to develop and maintain an ethos which places a better quality of life as the foremost mark of educational achievement and which emboldens all those attending their programmes to set high standards of corporate responsibility as the criteria of their official activities, whether commercial or governmental or in any other sphere. Growth is the catchword of the age and economic growth there must be whilst population increase and the extremes of wealth and poverty remain so stark. As Professor Dennis Gabor has said, 'we have absolutely nothing in our free economy that could ensure social stability at zero economic growth',[23] and I am afraid we have not travelled very far along the road towards the full integration of technological, human, social, cultural and economic values.

After visiting China last year Denis Healey wrote: 'What is unique is (their) unshakable determination to change human beings in their relations with one another rather than to achieve certain material goals,' and the central shift in priorities is 'towards moral rather than material incentivies, towards ideological rather than technical quality, towards community rather than individual values, towards co-operation rather than competition.'[24] In the first of these Stockton Lectures, Peter Walker drew our attention to the changing emphasis in the struggle between capitalism and Marxism. 'In a democratic society such as our own,' he said, 'those who advocate the advantages of a free enterprise system have as part of their aspirations a range of social objectives shared by many of the more enlightened people in communist countries.'

The ends we all seek are the same, but the means for achieving them are different. We are grateful to Eli Goldston and to the London Business School for the opportunity to range across the scene in search of remedies appropriate to our free enterprise way of life in the West.

NOTES

1   Alfred Zimmern, *Learning & Leadership,* 1928.
2   'Management Education & Training needs of Industry' – a report by an FBI working party, June 1963.
3   Mr. Edward Heath MP, to the Society of Education Officers at Westminster Technical College, London, on 25 January 1973.
4   'Technology in a Liberal Education' – Presidential address by Mr. J.C. Dancy to Section L (Education) on 2 September 1965, at the Cambridge Meeting of the British Association.
5   Quoted by *The Times*, 2 February 1973.
6   *The Times,* 18 January 1973.
7   *Financial Times,* 12 January 1973.
8   Capt. S.W. Roskill, *The Art of Leadership,* 1964.
9   'The British Elite', Thomas Balogh – BBC Radio 3, 20 January 1973.
10 Mr. Edward Heath, op. cit.
11 *The Listener,* 2 November 1972.
12 Oxford University Gazette, Supplement (2) to No. 3519, Wednesday 11 October 1972.
13 Birkbeck Foundation Oration 1972 by Sir Kenneth Berrill, 'Lifetime Education – The Outlook in Britain'.
14 'Education: A Framework for Expansion', Cmnd. 5714, HMSO, London, December 1972.
15 Mr. John Stoddart, assistant director of the North

East London Polytechnic, in *The Times Higher Education Supplement*, 1 December 1972.

16 Sir Kenneth Berrill, op. cit.

17 *The Listener*, op. cit.

18 Sir Kenneth Berrill, op. cit.

19 Mr. Paul Derrick in *The Times*, 28 December 1972.

20 *The Times*, 4 January 1973.

21 'The Social Sciences in the Great Debate on Science Policy', Andrew Shonfield *Minerva*, Vol. X, No. 3, July 1972.

22 '50 Million Volunteers' – a report on the role of Voluntary Organisations and Youth in the Environment, presented in February 1972 to the Secretary of State for the Environment.

23 'The Proper Priorities of Science & Technology', the 18th Fawley Foundation Lecture delivered at the University of Southampton by Professor Dennis Gabor FRS, 16 November 1972.

24 Mr. Denis Healey MP, *Sunday Times*, 12 November 1972.

SIX

Social Capitalism

P. WALKER

The Government is committed to securing more rapid
and sustained economic growth. The importance of this
commitment, however, is not a commitment to growth
for its own sake but a commitment to growth so that we
shall be able to obtain the improvements we want to see
in our society, and indeed to make a fuller contribution
to improving the quality of life throughout the world.

Growth in national output is easy to measure. It is
far more difficult to measure the improvement in the
quality of life. The Stockton Lectures have provided us
with a suitable forum to debate some of the emerging
problems of a modern industrial society. These lectures
demonstrate the nature of the choices that will be made
by Governments and by people in the period ahead.

In my opening lecture I commented upon the fact
that the capitalist and the Communist often have in mind
similar ends. There is also an increasing tendency for
Communist countries to apply means more associated
with capitalist concepts. Communist societies have come
to realise that they cannot do without the concept of a
rate of interest, that this concept is not simply a product
of 'bourgeois economics' but an essential part of rational
decision-taking. Indeed, the history of the economies of

119

Eastern Europe since the 1960s is very largely the story
of their discovery of the virtues of the once-despised
price mechanism and of the decentralised decision-taking.
It is therefore a mistake to think that the price system is
necessarily associated only with a capitalist society. It
can, and should be brought into play by every society
which seeks to secure an efficient allocation of resources.

Where capitalist and Communist societies differ is in
the way in which they organise economic life in their
attempt to deploy these common means more efficiently.
The question which we have to consider is – does a
centralised or state-planned system succeed in deploying
the means more efficiently than a system of private
enterprise?

There is no sense in denying that a socialist centrally
planned society can have certain advantages in allocating
resources efficiently; in particular, such a society may be
able to relate prices more closely to marginal cost than a
capitalist society. But a capitalist society will un-
doubtedly have two important, inter-connected and
overwhelming advantages, the advantages of innovation
and flexibility.

The advantage of innovation is a crucial one since the
problem of resource allocation is not static. We are not
merely asking how existing resources should be allocated
at lowest cost, but also whether our present methods and
techniques are more efficient than others which might be
adopted. To be able to answer this latter question we
need to look at the results of alternative techniques.

A society organised on socialist lines is likely to be
inherently hostile to innovation and risk-taking, hostile to
a situation where future discounted costs and receipts
cannot be worked out by a computer, but are at issue

between alternative and untried methods and techniques. In his recent book *Capitalism and the Permissive Society,* Samuel Brittan remarks upon the dowdiness and lack of imagination of the economies of Eastern Europe. Their use of the price mechanism has been an improvement upon previous 'socialist' methods of resource allocation; but the will to innovate does not exist in central investment boards. It seems that innovation requires a diversity of lending institutions and a diversity of means for obtaining private capital; such means are characteristic of capitalist societies; and therefore capitalist societies tend to display a positive attitude to innovation, and centrally-organised societies are more likely to display a conservative attitude to risk-taking.

In a socialist society political leadership decides upon major objectives and commits the resources of the nation totally to those objectives thus eliminating any scope for a different use of resources and, therefore, any scope for innovation. A socialist society also tends to have all of the disadvantages of large scale centrally-directed organisations. Indeed capitalism is increasingly suffering from a limiting of innovation as the scale of corporate bodies within the capitalist system increases and those of us who are conscious of the benefits of capitalism must be concerned about the dangers of creating industrial structures similar in magnitude and in the dominance of central direction to industrial organisations in socialist societies.

The dilemma of public ownership remains – either there is political control, when the public agency will be averse to risk and to the application of proper economic criteria; or alternatively managers will be free to act in accordance with economic criteria and all semblance of political control and public accountability will be lost.

The second overwhelming advantage of a society organised on the principles of private enterprise is its flexibility. It is misleading in many ways to speak of capitalism and socialism as if they were polar opposites. For whereas socialism represents a fixed, unchanging method of organising economic life, capitalism is remarkable by virtue of its ever-changing character. The capitalism of today is qualitatively very different from the capitalism of the early 1950s, let along the capitalism of the inter-war period.

The reason for this flexibility is that capitalism has been able to adopt a piecemeal, *ad hoc* approach to its problems. The central characteristic of socialist thought, on the other hand, is, in Popperian terms, its 'holism', its attempts to reorganise the whole structure of society to cure particular evils.

The original socialist criticism of capitalist society was that it could not solve the problem of poverty. Only by a wholesale reorganisation of industrial life would it be possible to provide sufficient for all. Then in the inter-war years it was said that capitalism inevitably involved large-scale unemployment. Socialists in the inter-war period were unable to accept the validity of the Keynesian hypothesis because they were unable to believe that unemployment would be cured within a capitalist framework. Ramsay MacDonald's Second Labour Government collapsed amid financial ruin because it was unwilling to deal with solutions within a capitalist framework, solutions which it regarded as mere 'tinkering', palliatives, while for them the fundamental question of industrial ownership was ignored. Today environmental and spillover effects resulting from economic growth are similarly said to be beyond the scope of capitalism to alleviate; it is said that we cannot have genuine corporate responsibility or employee participation in industry unless we alter the fundamental character of our economic life.

Harold Macmillan in his book *The Middle Way* published in 1938 realised that capitalism was not a fixed and unchanging method of organising economic life, but was far more adaptable than even some of its most sophisticated defenders realised. Macmillan argues that Keynesian remedies and planning policies could be used to deal with unemployment, while the essential nature of capitalism – its reliance on private risk-taking – would remain unchanged. Later on Macmillan attempted to introduce planning measures to deal, not with resource allocation as the Labour Government's post-war measures had done, but with the macro-economic problems of growth and incomes. Keynes and Macmillan can be regarded therefore as the intellectual progenitors of the modern mixed-economy capitalist society in which we now live. The moderate Right has been able to appreciate the rationale of such a society much more rapidly than the Left, because it has been able to see that planning is compatible with capitalism, more quickly than socialists have been able to see that the price mechanism is essential to efficient socialism.

This defence of capitalism, unlike the Friedmanite defence based upon the supremacy of *laissez-faire,* is essentially a moderate one. It implies, of course, regulatory intervention by the Government to secure full employment and control inflation. But the role of Government in a modern capitalist economy must be far wider than this.

For it is the duty of Government to define the social ends which private industry is to pursue. Such a function of Government is implicit in Lord Zuckerman's lecture and in much modern thinking concerning the functions of Government.

Social ends cannot be defined for us by technology and economics which are both sciences connected with the efficiency of means rather than the determination of ends. Nor, in the modern world can the national interest be determined by the result of the totally unregulated play of market forces. Milton Friedman has said that the free man 'recognised no national purpose except as it is the consensus of the purposes for which the citizens severally strive', but this amounts to saying that the national purpose is nothing more than a mere aggregation of selfish aims. Such a conception could never secure the ethical allegiance of more than a very small number of citizens; and without a more secure moral basis than that no structure of society can survive.

The Government has many functions to perform in a modern capitalist society. It has a duty to pursue economic policies that will enable economic growth to take place. It has to ensure that in a mixed economy such as our own, productive capacity is available. It has a considerable role to perform to see that the nature of the British economy is such as to gain the fullest benefits from the predicted pattern of world trade.

After rigorous analysis it has to set out aims for the quality of the physical environment and the preservation of the natural environment. It has to decide upon the proportion of resources to be allocated to the social services. It has to provide an educational system that not only enriches men's minds throughout their lives but positively provides an equality of opportunity.

It is, as Professor Beesley implies, a complete misconception to imagine that the role of Government in a modern industrial society is to manage industry. Rather its energies are to be concentrated upon stating social goals and, above all, upon backing up this statement by quantitative social cost benefit analysis.

The role of industry in terms of the above conception of the duties of Government must be seen not in terms of fulfilling them most efficiently. Competition is to be valued, not because the free play of competitive forces leads automatically to social welfare (it doesn't), but rather because competition decides who can fulfil the social needs set by Government most efficiently – which techniques and methods are likely to be the most successful. For it is precisely in this area that private enterprise is likely to prove most effective – by, in Professor Beesley's words 'translating ideals into effective action'.

This then is a new 'middle way' defence of capitalism involving neither of the extremes of complete centralisation on the one hand, or a Friedmanite Utopia on the other. Rather the function of the State is delineated in a spirit similar to that adopted by Keynes in the last chapter of the *General Theory* dealing with the social philosophy implied by the Keynesian theory of employment. The functions of the State, in such a scheme, must amount to far more than merely 'holding the ring'; rather the state must be responsible for the central strategic decisions of the modern economy; leaving to industry the tactical fulfilment of these decisions.

The central weakness of modern capitalism is that, despite its outstanding success in securing material improvement without precedent in human history, as well as a degree of personal liberty for all, unknown to previous generations, it has been unable to generate ideological commitment. Few really accept the kind of defence outlined above; capitalism is accepted in this country because of the innate conservatism of the British people and because other alternatives seem far worse, rather than because of any positive allegiance to the system.

Such a situation is to be deplored since the ultimate basis of support for any social system must always be its general acceptance as a morally justified system. The strength of socialism has always been its idealistic appeal. That is why injustices and inequalities in socialist societies are less subject to attack than similar injustices in capitalist societies. Where the fundamental ideology is felt to be sound, deviations from it are not regarded in such a serious light.

What are the reasons for the failure of capitalism to capture the popular imagination? I can suggest three.

1. The proud claim of capitalism that it produces equality of opportunity is often honoured more in the breach than the observance. Too often the distinctions of heredity and class are allowed to obscure merit. If a capitalist society wishes to obtain moral authority it must be ruthless in securing equality of opportunity.

2. Those who, in a capitalist society, possess superior power and privilege, are felt often not to justify these in terms of superior performance.

3. Holders of corporate power in capitalist society are often seen as insufficiently socially responsible. They are thought, rightly or wrongly, as

insufficiently concerned with the environment, with justice to their employees, and with justice to those belonging to a different race. Companies must be seen to have a far more genuine social conscience before capitalism is regarded as a virtuous, as opposed to a merely efficient method of organising economic life. It is no good saying that the only responsibility of companies is to maximise their profits; for men need to see some connection between their own moral values and the central institutions of the society of their values if they are to command their allegiance.

It is the failure to secure such values which renders capitalism so insecure ideologically. As compared both with feudal and with socialist societies, a capitalist society is peculiarly susceptible to a lack of moral authority. This is because of its emphasis on freedom and self-dependence, and its reliance on rational authority unsupported by religion. This lack of a central moral substance leads only too easily to nihilism; and this is indeed a predominant attitude amongst many of the articulate young.

In his lecture, Mr. Nind refers to other problems which he supposes to be problems peculiarly associated with capitalism but which are, I believe, problems associated with any industrial society that has reached our present stage of industrial and technological development. The combination of large-scale institutions, an extreme division of labour, and a complex superstructure of technical knowledge, are bound to lead to alienation regardless of how economic life is organised. Many of the defects Marx saw as inherent in capitalism are in reality evils of industrial society as such.

Mr. Nind, however, rightly sees as one of the central problems of a society such as capitalism, with its denial of innate differences between men, a conflict between the increasing complexities and technicalities of modern industrial society, and a democratic ethic asserting equality. It is for this reason he says that men feel frustrated and unhappy; they are unable to understand the processes which govern their lives. They see themselves as passive victims – 'Us' against 'Them' – even when 'They' are applying beneficial reforms.

It is vital that the structure of administration be made more rational and comprehensible to the people. They should be told in clear terms the basis for Government action. So far most capitalist societies have been unable to develop the rapport with the people which is essential if their allegiance is to be obtained. The failure to communicate is a failure both on the part of Government and of industry. The failure has perhaps resulted from the continuing mood of superiority by those who have had the power to take the bigger decisions – the relationship between baron and serf continued between landowner and tenant and still sometimes continued between industrialist and worker – perhaps best illustrated by the nineteenth century phrases of 'master and men'. We are a long way from giving the full opportunity of developing and then applying the full ability of each individual. For too many the bulk of their lives is determined by the domestic environment in which they were originally born or by the education that was made available to them in the first quarter of their lives. For too many an early opportunity missed results in a life wasted.

Our aim is the creation of a civilised society. It is an

aim that requires the eradication of much misery that already exists. It will also require the creation of a society in which all of the people have a share in the happiness and dignity of life itself. We have much progress to make before we attain that civilised society.

Notes on Contributors

Michael Beesley is Professor of Economics at the London Graduate School of Business Studies.

Philip Nind is Director of the Foundation for Management Education.

Peter Walker is Secretary of State, Department of Trade and Industry.

Lord Zuckerman is Chairman of the Commission on Mining and the Environment.

Index